EDMUND BURKE

AMS PRESS
NEW YORK

EDMUND BURKE

and the

Revolt against the Eighteenth Century

*A Study of the Political and Social Thinking of
Burke, Wordsworth, Coleridge and Southey*

by

ALFRED COBBAN

M.A., Ph.D.

*Lecturer in History, Armstrong College, in the
University of Durham*

LONDON
GEORGE ALLEN & UNWIN LTD
MUSEUM STREET

Library of Congress Cataloging in Publication Data

Cobban, Alfred.
    Edmund Burke and the revolt against the
eighteenth century.

    Reprint of the 1929 ed. published by G. Allen
& Unwin, London.
    Bibliography: p.
    Includes index.
    1. Political science—Great Britain—History.
2. Burke, Edmund, 1729?-1797—Political science.
3. Eighteenth century. 4. Wordsworth, William,
1770-1850—Political and social views.
5. Coleridge, Samuel Taylor, 1772-1834—Political
and social views. 6. Southey, Robert, 1774-
1843—Political and social views. I. Title.
JA84.G7C6   1978   320.5'092'2   75-28995
ISBN 0-404-14006-8

First AMS edition published in 1978.

Reprinted from the edition of 1929, London, from an
original in the collections of the University of Chicago
Library. [Trim size of the original has been slightly altered
in this edition. Original trim size: 12 x 18.9 cm. Text area
of the original has been maintained in this edition. Original
text area: 8.9 x 14.6 cm.]

MANUFACTURED
IN THE UNITED STATES OF AMERICA

TO

MY MOTHER

PREFACE

THE PREPARATION OF THIS BOOK was commenced while I was studying Burke under the supervision of Dr. H. W. V. Temperley of Peterhouse, Cambridge, to whom I am greatly indebted. I am also very grateful to Professor J. Lyle Morison of Armstrong College for much encouragement and kindness, and to my wife, whose assistance greatly lightened the burden of preparing the book for publication. For the leisure which allowed of its writing I am indebted to the grant of a Research Scholarship by Gonville and Caius College, Cambridge.

Part of the material for Chapter IV has been published in the *Cambridge Historical Journal*, Vol. II, No. I, under the title, *Edmund Burke and the Origins of the Theory of Nationality*.

Considerations of space have made it necessary to give only those references which seem the more important and interesting. I have in general referred to the most easily obtainable editions.

CONTENTS

EDMUND BURKE

CHAPTER I

FUNDAMENTAL IDEAS
OF THE EIGHTEENTH CENTURY

THE EIGHTEENTH CENTURY has been called
"the seed-time of modern Europe". To a student of
political history such a judgment on the age extending
roughly from 1688 to 1789 might well appear strange.
Standing between two periods of rapid and fundamental
change, such as were the seventeenth and nineteenth
centuries, the intervening years might seem to the casual
observer of the historic scene an age during which the
development of Europe halted for a while. One cannot
pretend that it was a peaceful or uneventful period which
saw the long struggle between England and France, the
rise of Prussia and Russia, the decline of older Powers,
and the beginning of that redrawing of the map of Europe
which the next century carried so far. But not only was
the heart of the period, the generation of Walpole and
Fleury, a breathing-space, but even the wars of this
century stand on a different footing from those of the
preceding and following ages. Whereas the seventeenth
century struggled over fundamental questions of religion
and internal government and the nineteenth was rent
by the aspirations of nations and classes, the political
history of the eighteenth century is almost entirely
concerned with the territorial aggrandizement of States
and the ambitions of rulers. It is little exaggeration to

say that, apart from changes in the relative power of States, the Europe of 1789 was to outward appearance the Europe of the Peace of Westphalia.

After 1789, on the other hand, the old order changes at a cataclysmic pace. There is no denying that the placid waters of the eighteenth century led straight to the cataracts of revolution—and a revolution that was not merely the overthrow of a government but the destruction of a whole ancient order of society, and the emergence of forces and ideas of social life whose existence had not been recognized before. Now a vast revolution such as this does not arise out of nothing: its roots are deep in the past, and its slow subterranean growth can be traced, even though it be among the most obscure and least noticed events of preceding generations. This is manifestly true of the French Revolution, and it explains why the eighteenth century can be described as the "seed-time of modern Europe". For the French Revolution is the eighteenth century in action. The ideas which governed the Revolution are the ideas evolved by the century, and the same ideas, expressed in the Revolution, dominated the subsequent age. Thus, a chaotic *mêlée*, void of meaning in the world of politics, in the world of thought the eighteenth century can justly be considered the great formative age of modern Europe.

Its ideas guided the Revolution, they are the ideas on which the nineteenth century has lived. But they are also the ideas with which the twentieth century is becoming dissatisfied; for the rule of the eighteenth-century system of social and political ideas is at last being seriously challenged. A catastrophe of such colossal dimensions as the world suffered in the world war and the series of revolutions which accompanied it, cannot occur without

12

undermining to some extent men's faith in accepted ideas. The simple optimism of the *Aufklärung* and the lesser Victorians is not for a post-war generation. As Burke wrote in a former time of trouble: "New things in a new world! I see no hope in the common tracks." Yet the only real alternatives offered to-day seem to be violent and unconstructive, willing to destroy the existing achievements of Western civilization and put nothing in their place, to revert from the age of rationalism and middle-class democracy to the ages of tyranny and blind faith. The world needs instead a constructive effort to remould institutions to suit altered conditions and re-establish Western civilization on sounder intellectual bases. What is needed, too, is not an ingenious twisting of accepted ideas to new conclusions, but a re-thinking of the fundamentals of individual and social life.

For this purpose any system of ideas differing from the prevailing may offer a useful corrective. Some modern thinkers have gone to the Greeks, some to the Middle Ages. But there is one source of ideas in some respects more valuable than either. It is too often forgotten that at the very moment of triumph of the *Aufklärung* there was developing a movement based on essentially hostile principles and involving a conscious and definite revolt against the existing trend of ideas. This movement, represented in England first and foremost by Burke, then by the "Lake Poets"—Wordsworth, Coleridge, and Southey—together with such incidental allies as Scott, Landor, and Cobbett, is the subject of our study. For the history of thought it is only confusing to take all the romanticists as belonging to one school; while to forget the close relationship of the ideas of the Lake Poets to those of their great predecessor, Burke, is fatal. Hence to call this the Romantic Movement would be misleading, because that term as generally used in literary history includes writers of the second generation of romanticism, such as Byron and Shelley, whose affiliations in political thinking are far more with the *philosophes* and the eighteenth-century tradition than with Wordsworth and Coleridge.

After the first force of the revolt against the eighteenth century had spent itself, its ideas were reasserted with undiminished vigour. Although, however, the revolt had failed, it remains of permanent value as a constructive criticism of ideas which still direct the course of civilization. Before we can study it, though, a necessary preliminary is to discover the nature of those eighteenth-century ideas against which certain of the romantics, like our own generation, were revolting: this must be the subject of our first chapter.

I

THE SENSATIONAL PSYCHOLOGY AND ITS CONSEQUENCES

When we talk of the eighteenth century as a separate era in the history of thought, how do we distinguish it from those that came before and after? The preceding period is obviously the age of the Reformation, with constitutional and religious strife raging in every country, warring systems of rights ranged against one another, Catholic, Lutheran, and Calvinist churches and sects struggling for their own predominance and the suppression of their rivals, aristocracy and the divine right monarchy waging war to the death, but turning now and again to face occasional outbursts of popular anarchy. And in the midst of all these struggles we find the fundamentals of thought accepted by practically every party. Despite the classical revival, despite Descartes, in essence the mediaeval conception of life is still intact. Divine sanction, of one party or another, is still the criterion in politics, while the theological conception of the universe has been challenged by few and by none successfully. Pass to the nineteenth century and we find an almost complete secularization of life, which has reduced theology to a specialized activity unconnected with everyday life. The Western world is concerned with material progress and national aggrandizement, not merely in practice—the sixteenth century had been sufficiently materialistic in fact—but also in theory. It naturally follows that whereas the theoretic world of theology and mathematics had been the preoccupation of thinkers in the seventeenth century, thinkers of the nineteenth century tended to pay more attention to the experiential world of physical science and history. Our object in this chapter is to discover the essential ideas of the age that came between, during which the transition must have occurred.

Psychology, it has been said, was not invented when Shakespeare wrote *Hamlet*; nevertheless in all periods the foundation of thought is the prevailing theory of psychology. What a man thinks about himself is after all the most important factor in determining what he will think about the world as a whole, and in this sense man is the measure of all things. This is important for us, because man as conceived by the eighteenth century was a very peculiar creature; as an actual phenomenon he was not studied at all, but a theory about him was taken from the writer whose influence pervades the eighteenth century with an almost scriptural authority. It has been called the century of revolt against authority, of reckless scepticism, yet surely never has a secular writer obtained such universal recognition or been received with such unquestioning faith as Locke. For a hundred years Europe contrived to live on his ideas, modifying and developing them in all directions, but making no fundamental change. Now Locke himself had quite definitely given psychology the priority over all other studies. His ideal for the student was to substitute observation for authority by working on the empirical method vaguely adumbrated by Bacon, but he admits that there is this preliminary question: before we can understand the world of experience we must examine the instrument by which we come to know it and satisfy ourselves concerning the validity of our knowledge.(1) In other words we must begin with the epistemological problem—the problem of knowledge. But beginning thus by studying the mind as an instrument by which knowledge is acquired and accumulated, he tends to assume that it can be nothing more than a mere instrument for a mechanical recording of experiences. Then, if the mind is only a mechanism it naturally follows that the important question Locke has to ask himself is always—what is experienced, never—what experiences. The conclusion of the argument, and the first postulate of his *Essay on the Human Understanding*, is therefore that all knowledge is purely empirical.

Hence he is committed to a direct denial of the Cartesian doctrine of innate ideas and devotes his first chapter to its disproval. For him the mind is "white paper, void of all characters, without any ideas", when it comes into being. The problem is how comes the writing on the blank sheet of the mind. "How comes it to be furnished? Whence comes it by that vast store which the busy and boundless fancy of man has painted on it, with an almost endless variety? Whence has it all the materials of reason and knowledge? To this I answer in one word, from experience; in that all our knowledge is founded; and from that it ultimately derives itself. Our observation, employed either about external sensible objects, or about the internal operations of our minds, perceived and reflected on by ourselves, is that which supplies our understandings with all the materials of thinking. These two are the fountains of knowledge, from whence all the ideas we have, or can naturally have, do spring."(2) All our simple ideas, that is, come from experience, and all complex ideas are formed out of the simple by the process of reflection. This latter process, the formation of complex ideas, contains an implication that the mind has an active part to play in the organization of human knowledge, which would make Locke's own position not so very different from that enshrined by Leibnitz in the terms of his famous compromise: *nihil in intellectu quod non prius in sensu, nisi intellectus ipse*. But it is needless to discuss this possible qualification of Locke's empiricism, since it was to be obscured by the more striking theories of later speculators, whose cruder empiricism came to pass for psychological orthodoxy and the pure milk of Lockian doctrine.

There were among those who followed in the wake of Locke two genuine philosophers and a host of charlatans. Certain inconsistencies of which he had been guilty were revealed by Berkeley and Hume. Berkeley exposed the inadequacy of Locke's attempt to explain away the existence of universals, or, as he called them, abstract ideas, though his own solution of the problem can hardly be called much more successful. He emphasizes even more than Locke the view that the mind is nothing but a congeries of sense perceptions, whose only being is to be perceived; from which he is led on to postulate a Deity as the only means of importing unity and permanence into the universe. But the view of reality which was to him the merest common sense was wildest paradox to most of his contemporaries. Coxcombs having vanquished Berkeley with a grin, and the attempt of the learned and imaginative Bishop of Cloyne to draw the empirical psychology to theistic and even to semi-idealistic conclusions having thus proved abortive, it was left for Hume to take up the task of working out Locke's half-finished empiricism to its logical conclusions.

Hume, like Berkeley, pushes his denial of the mind's power of originality farther than Locke did, and refuses to admit even reflection as a factor in the making of ideas. Faced in consequence with the problem of explaining the formation of complex out of simple ideas, that is, sense data, alone, he brings in a suggestion which Locke had thrown out casually and proceeds to make it the essential principle of mental operations. Association of ideas, a mechanical process by which one idea gets linked to another, becomes for him the open sesame to psychological truth. The mind consists, according to Hume, of a series of presentations, perceptions or sense data, which by becoming associated in various ways form all our ideas. Why they should be associated in any particular way rather than any other he never explains properly, and indeed the putting together of the mind and its knowledge

18

by Hume is so much less successful than his preliminary pulling to pieces that his name has become identified with the extremest scepticism. He himself was driven to deny that rationalism could provide a sound basis for psychology, and passed on to politics and ethics, in which spheres his ruthless logic wrought with equally devastating effect on contemporary ideas.

Hume and Berkeley, however, though after Locke the only two philosophers worthy of the name belonging to the empirical school, and important because they exhaust its possibilities and prepare the way for Kant, were prevented, the one by his scepticism, and the other by his paradoxes, from exercising any noteworthy influence over their contemporaries. A cruder empiricism dominated the lesser minds of the *Aufklärung* and took its best known form in the *Traité des sensations* (1754) of Condillac, with its absurd statue analogy. Condillac supposes a statue contrived in every detail as a man but lacking mentality or senses. Then he imagines the five senses bestowed one by one on the statue, and traces the resulting development of mind until a complete human psychology has been evolved.

Into the absurdities to which the sensational psychology led there is no need to penetrate, however, the important question is what were its consequences on thought, and these proved far more extensive and profound than the superficial nature of the philosophy would lead one to suspect. The sensational psychology involved, in the first place, a strictly mechanistic view of the universe and man, for a frank admittal of which we have to go to such works as La Mettrie's *L'Homme Machine* or d'Holbach's *Système de la Nature*. "Man", says La Mettrie, "is but an animal made up of a number of springs, which are all put in motion by each other."(3) Exposed in its naked crudity, the materialism of the dominant psychological creed revolted public opinion and made a by-word of the names of these writers, who yet were only guilty of proclaiming openly conclusions which any orthodox psychologist of the day should have accepted. What room was there in the system of Locke for any but material forces? Was it possible for anything creative to come from the mind of Condillac's statue? Accepting this view, was not Voltaire justified in his mockery of the old prejudice that there was somehow attached to the human body something not material, something that might be called a soul? It required no such hypothesis to account for the Lockian mind, which could easily be explained as a resultant of the material universe, a mirror peculiar in being itself both see-er and seen, created in the first place by that universe which it subsequently reflected. For apart from the picture of the world what was to be found there? Only the mirror itself, a simple mechanism, a mere nothing.

Not all the eighteenth-century thinkers were sufficiently strong stomached to stand the implications of their own beliefs, but in one degree or another they all gravitated towards materialism. As a philosophy their scheme of things was beneath contempt, but it satisfied the men of the Enlightenment, who, indeed, were as little philosophical as any who have ever arrogated to themselves the term. In fact, Berkeley and Hume, together with Diderot, were perhaps the only *philosophes* of the Lockian school who have any right to the name. For the rest, they were empiricists and confined themselves to the world of external experience. The age of reason was bitterly hostile to rationalism: it broke completely with the

Platonic tradition. *"O Platon tant admiré"*, cries Voltaire, *"vous n'avez conté que des fables."*(4) And with Plato went all real philosophy; Vico and Spinoza might never have lived. "Let us then follow the direction of experience and not trouble our heads with the vain history of philosophers", advises the arch-materialist, La Mettrie.(5) "The direction of experience"—what a host of unrealized corollaries lies in that phrase. But the eighteenth century thought it had proceeded as far as was necessary when it had appealed to experience, the teaching of which could easily be discovered by the unprejudiced observer. The age of reason might much better have been called the age of *bon sens*: common sense was to be the guide of life and the criterion of philosophic truth, and phenomena which it could not explain it could at least explain away. Locke's sensational psychology provided an admirable framework for that common-sense view of things in general which took the place of a philosophy for his disciples.

The truth is that if we judge Locke and his successors as philosophers we are necessarily unfair to them. One cannot help suspecting that the philosophical issue was of the least importance to Locke. He decrees the non-existence of innate ideas, for instance, not so much because they represent a philosophically unsound theory as because they are a nuisance. Frankly unwilling to put out on the "vast ocean of being", he acknowledges at the very beginning of his inquiry the narrow limits of the human intellect, and for the rest of his not very adventurous philosophic voyage confines himself to coasting well in sight of the firm land of common sense, applying the telescope, with a pertinacity worthy of a bolder cause, always to the blind eye when it points seaward. But this

21

indifference on the part of the *philosophes* to ultimate problems is not the result of mere laziness; it arises out of their keen interest in the practical problems of life and conduct. "*O homme*," says Voltaire, "*ce Dieu t'a donné l'entendement pour te bien conduire, et non pour pénétrer dans l'essence des choses qu'il a créées.*"(6) They refused to worry themselves over Descartes's innate ideas, Spinoza's God, Leibnitz's monads or Plato's ideas, still less over the rigmarole of the schoolmen, because they saw so much folly, wickedness and misery in the world that might be prevented by taking thought on less elevated subjects.

The reason why remarkably little speculation on social life had gone on in modern Europe before Locke is not far to seek. Thinking in the Middle Ages had been almost a clerical monopoly, and right up to the end of the seventeenth century, except for a few isolated individuals, European thought retained its theological colouring. Now this was important, because mediaeval Christianity concentrated attention on the other world and looked for little improvement in the affairs of this we live in. The Reformation worked no beneficial change in this respect, for if anything the Lutheran doctrine of redemption by faith derogated still farther from the importance of works, sufficiently discouraged as they were already by a tendency to trust in Providence. We know, of course, that the idea of progress was not present in the mediaeval mind, but the trouble, more than that, was that it had not even occurred to men that they could, by taking thought systematically, bring about improvement in conditions of life. Any change, it was felt, was likely to be·for the worse. The world-view of the Middle Ages was essentially pessimistic. Progress, whether in the realm of thought or in the realm of external facts, was not possible because it was not considered desirable, and it was considered undesirable because in any real sense impossible. The mind¦ of Europe was involved in a vicious circle from which there was only one way out. That was to free the whole problem from the fetters of theological argument, and build up a system of thought on entirely new bases, unconnected with any religious system.

The Renaissance began the work of secularizing thought. Descartes established a rationalism which for a time carried all before it. But the thinking of the Cartesians was for the most part confined to logic and mathematics, and by the beginning of the eighteenth century seemed to have lost its vitality. Inferior as a philosophy, the system of Locke had greater practical merits, though Locke himself only proceeded half-way towards the emancipation of thought from the incubus of theological presupposition. He can still say, "It is rational to conclude, that our proper employment lies in those inquiries, and in that sort of knowledge which is most suited to our natural capacities, and carries in it our greatest interest, i.e. the condition of our eternal estate"; whilst he is pessimistic concerning the progress of scientific knowledge: "We are able, I imagine, to reach very little general knowledge concerning the species of bodies, and their several properties." But here he is mainly safeguarding science against the application of a deductive method, for he continues, "All that I would say is . . . that we should not take doubtful systems for complete sciences. . . . In the knowledge of bodies, we must be content to glean what we can from particular experiments; since we cannot, from a discovery of their real essences, grasp at a time whole sheaves; and in bundles comprehend the nature and properties of whole species together."(7) In spite of the claims of Bacon or da Vinci, Locke and his disciples must be accounted the true founders of inductive science and the first to exploit the empirical outlook.

The importance of empiricism was that it turned men for the first time to the study of phenomena independent of any preconceived opinions and prejudices. That was a great advance and conferred benefits on the human race more than sufficient to make amends for the temporary denial of higher values that it may be thought to have involved. For it was only a short step from the study of actual human conditions to speculation on their improvement, and here again Locke's psychological theory proved of the greatest value. The psychology of the *tabula rasa*, absurdly mistaken as it was, played an essential part in the development of modern thought. If man is given us at birth packed full of innate principles, inexorable instincts, inborn traditions, it is obvious that little fresh can be made of him; he will live and die precisely as his fathers lived and died, and any attempt to alter or improve his lot is doomed to disappointment. Sweeping away the whole accepted theory of man at a blow, Locke presents us with an entirely different situation, in which man's mind when he is born is no more than a sheet of blank paper whereon we may write what we will. No more revolutionary doctrine has ever been put forward, for by it most obviously education and environment become lord and master of man, and it is possible to change the whole face of society in a single generation. Progress has ceased to be a dream and has become a practical issue. Although other intellectual forces went to the formation of the idea of progress, without the assistance given by

24

the sensational psychology the idea could never have achieved the prominence and general acceptance that it did towards the end of the eighteenth century.

II

NATURAL LAW

To accept the possibility of continuous progress as a result of rational endeavour, though in itself a step important enough to mark a new epoch, was only the first step: it was next necessary to determine the conditions under which progress could take place. In the Middle Ages the duty of laying down the fundamental laws of social life had been the function of religion, but religion had fallen on hard times in the eighteenth century. After two hundred years of religious strife the dogmas and intolerances of the churches were going out of fashion with the educated classes. Out of the reliques of mediaeval Christianity had been evolved in England a kind of rational religion which was called deism. In the land of its birth it did not long enjoy a separate existence, and in the course of about fifty years the pure milk of Anglicanism had been watered down sufficiently by the thinner liquid of common sense to prove palatable to the majority of deists. The few who did not return to the fold followed Hume down the road to scepticism. But while deism was declining in England it was starting a triumphant career in France, under the auspices of the writer who was to prove the greatest literary force Europe has ever known. Deism became a new movement when

Voltaire set up as its prophet. He took it up, perhaps, not so much because of intellectual conviction as on account of the incidental advantages of a faith that formed a defence against the charge of atheism without involving acceptance of any particular creed, that furnished an ideally flexible lay figure to be decked in any old clothes the controversialist desired, and that could always be appealed to as a basis for morals and sanction for politics. Deism thus provided all the useful services of Christianity at a much cheaper rate and with fewer drafts on credulity. No more was to be asked: Voltaire's God has been called a celestial gendarme. He instructs us, "*Nulle société ne peut subsister sans justice. Annonçons donc un Dieu juste*". "*Si la loi de l'état punit les crimes connus, annonçons donc un Dieu qui punira les crimes inconnus.*" The conclusion is plain, "*Qu'un philosophe soit spinosiste s'il veut; mais que le homme d'État soit théiste*".(1).

For the historian of thought deism is of little importance save as an ill-lighted and inhospitable half-way house between mediaeval Christianity and the philosophy of the Absolute. It was useful in its day because it provided a groundwork on which unity, sacrificed by the rejection of Catholic Christianity, could be rebuilt. Revealed religion had gone, it seemed, but the mind of man, though enfranchised, felt still the need of seeing the world as a whole; Providence had been moved out of the way, but the Laws of Nature remained; the highway to Heaven had fallen down to grass, but laws of the road were still felt to be an imperative necessity. More than that, although the dogmas of revealed religion, the commandments of a personal God, were no longer respected, instead of falling into chaos the world of thought had become much more disciplined, with the establishment of the theory of a

26

rigidly mechanistic universe governed by unvarying inexorable law. The fault of the *philosophes* was not that they allowed liberty to degenerate into licence, it was that they set up a mechanical universe in which liberty or free-will seemed to have no place at all: they were the Puritans of the intellect, and deism was only a means of asserting the rule of law.

Law, more particularly the Laws of Nature, which formed the positive content of deism, constituted the mould into which all their ideas were cast. Deism, to use another analogy, was a convex mirror in which was concentrated in pale and unsubstantial fashion the thought of the age. Especially did it reflect the scientific conquests, which in their turn deepened and clarified the conception of law. How great was the revolution effected by the discoveries of Newton is shown by such a pre-Newtonian observation as Locke's, "The works of nature are contrived by a wisdom, and operate by ways, too far surpassing our faculties to discover, or capacities to conceive, for us ever to be able to reduce them into a science".(2) Before Newton, deism was as lacking in scientific basis as orthodox Christianity. But his astronomical system seemed to provide a cosmological proof of a theistic world, which Voltaire welcomed in the name of deism and Addison hymned for the Anglican Church:

> The spacious firmament on high,
> With all the blue ethereal sky,
> And spangled heavens, a shining frame,
> Their great Original proclaim.

Nature became the clock, from which one argued back to the clockmaker, God. Deism and the Law of Nature confirmed one another; and so it came about that the *philosophes* took for their main task the discovery of natural laws.

These laws were, it must be kept in mind, the fundamental rules which governed human progress, extending over the moral realm as well as over physical nature. Ethics were conceived in as thoroughly Newtonian a spirit as physics. Now an eighteenth-century law was by no means the scientific law or working hypothesis as it is conceived to-day. It was a peculiar and quite illegitimate hybrid of empiricism and rationalism; in it the deductive method, lately expelled with contumely by Locke's empiricism, returned triumphantly under the aegis of natural philosophy. For the branch of scientific study which had most influence on the *philosophes* was mathematical astronomy, which to the mind without scientific training might easily seem to follow a deductive method. Voltaire, as a dabbler in chemistry and a natural sceptic, inclined to shun general views, but most of the *philosophes* in their attempt to introduce the rule of law in other fields than that of physical science fell back on deduction. In fact their laws of nature were little more than chance guesses taken as universal principles. For instance, gravitation, the cement of the physical universe, was supposed to have analogous to it a law of reason, which held the moral world together; and as from the former we can deduce what any particular star or planet will do in given circumstances, so from the latter we can deduce what will be the conduct of a man in any particular situation. This law of reason was in effect but another name for the intellectualist psychology of Locke; it made the search for psychological laws very simple, since only the conscious layer of the mind need be taken into account and only actions capable of rational explanation. Was it not to be expected, now, that the

28

philosophes should achieve as marvellous results in their sphere as Newton in his? Alas, apart from the discovery and formulation of platitudes the search for the principles governing human relations did not prosper greatly; but it proved fruitful of results of supreme importance in two directions. In the one, Montesquieu and the Physiocrats in France, with Hume, Adam Smith and their successors in England, laid the foundations of classical economics. The other direction had been indicated by Locke and Hume, on whose pleasure-pain psychology was later to be based the whole moral and political doctrine of utilitarianism. Let us take these two in turn.

Going back as always to Locke for its beginnings, and greatly advanced by Hume and Montesquieu, the new attitude towards economic relations culminated in the schools headed by Quesnay in France and Adam Smith in England, the differences between which are for our purposes unimportant compared with their essential similarities. The doctrines of both schools bear many characteristic marks of the century which produced them. Their economic man is psychologically the creation of the *Essay on the Human Understanding*, a conscious, rational being whose head works on strictly intellectualist principles, and whose heart has been dissected into a series of moral aphorisms. He is conceived in the first place as the solitary inhabitant of a desert island, because in that situation the natural man is least liable to suffer the distorting effects of human society. From him are taken away all the variations and differences which go to make up the infinitely diverse human being of reality. The psychology of this abstract man is established *a priori* and his actions in various combinations of circumstances deduced from it. But we need not trouble ourselves

29

with the various laws discovered by this ingenious method, the faults of which were transcended by the greater economists but exaggerated by many of their disciples.

However, economics is a science of means, for ends we have to go to ethics, and here in the eighteenth century had taken place perhaps the most fundamental change of all, the adoption of a secular standpoint. Except for a few rather isolated individuals during the Renaissance, it is true to say that Locke was the first to write on ethics and politics in a pretty consistently un-theological manner. Now the essence of secularity is utilitarianism. So, good and evil, he says, are to be used only with reference to pleasure and pain—and with that saying utilitarianism springs into being.(3) The result is to enfranchise conduct from the laws of the theologians, but only in order to submit it to the laws of the *philosophes*; for their ethical principles were still deductive, still discovered by the "high priori" route. Not all eighteenth-century utilitarians followed Locke in the latter, however. Hume pushes the attack beyond theological ethics and directs it against all deductive ethics whatever, not only asserting that pain and pleasure are the mainsprings of human action, but practically making the whole essence of virtue and vice to reside in the tendency of actions to produce pleasure or pain.(4) There still remains the equivocation that this may be interpreted as meaning either pleasure and pain to some moral sense or as simple hedonism. Hume, inclining to the latter position, tends to equate the passions which influence the will with simple pleasure-pain feeling. More completely than any other eighteenth-century thinker does he abandon rationalism, and although "feeling", as it comes to fill in Hume's thought the place of reason, seems to adopt some of the leading characteristics of the dethroned monarch of the mind, his influence is thrown more heavily on the side of the ascendant naturalism, and narrows down to the particular form that was to triumph with the system of Helvétius and Bentham: Utilitarianism was the creed demanded by the age, and Hume was not the least among its prophets. Implicit right through Locke, it saturates the thought of the ensuing age, and if the names of Helvétius and Bentham are remembered more especially in this connection it is only because theirs were the most notable attempts at systematizing the vague general idea. In Bentham the eighteenth century finds the last and the greatest of its prophets.

To analyse in further detail these ideas would be to occupy more space for this preliminary chapter than is justified. The psychological theory, ethical principle, and general philosophy of life held by the dominant school of thinkers in the eighteenth century should by now be sufficiently indicated. It remains only to show what happened to this system of ideas towards the end of the century.

The true heirs of the Enlightenment were the philosophical radicals, classical economists, and middle-class reformers of nineteenth-century England. In France itself the movement was side-tracked, the *philosophes* proper, such as Diderot and d'Holbach, moving off to more extreme theories than Voltaire's and alienating sympathy. Meanwhile the star of Rousseau had risen on the literary horizon, and when it reached its meridian that dazzling luminary quite obscured the lesser lights of the *Aufklärung*. With Rousseau we reach to the Revolution and beyond to the Romantic movement, for that strange and contradictory personality was the prophet of romanticism on the one hand, and of the combination of utilitarian reform with the demand for individual rights which resulted in the Revolution, on the other. With the latter aspect of Rousseau—undoubtedly on that side of his mind a thinker belonging to the eighteenth century —we come to the synthesis and climax of the thought of the age. Rousseau, to whose mind inconsistency was no bugbear, was especially well suited to be the interpreter of an age which based itself on such a colossal inconsistency as the union of the assertion of individual right with a denial of individuality: for in fact the political ideals of the school of Locke amounted to the former and its psychological theories to the latter. While, as has been indicated above, attention was concentrated on a mechanical universe and its laws, interest in the individual had naturally declined; the "simple, separate person" as a force in the shaping of the world had been overlooked, his part in the causation of events forgotten, and he himself had come to be regarded just as a result, the product of the action of a set of mechanical laws on a material so purely passive, so lacking in qualities, and so undifferentiated, that it could hardly be said to exist at all. Yet this material was human nature. There were many facts which might have suggested otherwise, but they were disregarded: Locke's influence had given an authoritative cachet to the idea that men were by nature very much alike in all ages and all climes. Modern psychologists are disposed to agree that racial and other differences in the stuff of human nature, in the natural man, have been exaggerated, and to attribute more to the influence of the "social inheritance" than the nineteenth century was willing to. Certainly the *philosophes* in their quest of the natural man were on the track of an important truth, though their arguments suffered from their uncertainty

but we must distinguish between those which a
true sense novel and those which are merely develop
of typical eighteenth-century habits of thought.
examples of the former we may take nationality ⸴
socialism, of the latter, liberal democracy, the Concert ⸴
Europe, and the classical economy. The scope of these
latter movements is witness to the extended activity of
eighteenth-century principles on the succeeding century,
and indicates how largely subsequent historical development was dictated by ideas and tendencies set in operation
during what Dr. Arnold once described as "the great
misused seed-time of modern Europe". The optimistic,
utilitarian, and individualist world-view of the eighteenth
century, regardless that it had been partially undermined
in advance by the criticism of Hume, heedless of the efforts
of the Romanticists and the Idealists to build up rival
systems, dominated Great Britain in the succeeding
century with all the authority of a time-hallowed creed.
The other side of the picture, the latent pessimism and
scepticism in the sad world of *Candide*, was hardly
revealed to Europe at large until our own after-war years.

The world of common life usually lags behind the
world of thought even by a century or so, and a great
intellectual movement seldom enters into its kingdom
before it has come to lose all validity for the class of
professional thinkers with whom it originated. So it is,
one may suggest, that Europe has in these latter years
reached an outlook recalling in many ways that of the
more pessimistic and sceptical thinkers of the eighteenth
century. All the big guns and light artillery of the
Aufklärung, long disused, obsolete, stacked away out of
the light, and these not only in the form of the sober
conclusions of Hume and Voltaire, but of the wildest

as to what they meant by nature—an equivocal term susceptible of either a philosophical or an historical interpretation. Whatever Nature might mean, it was at any rate agreed that natural man was free from the artificial differences which kings and nobles and priests have imposed on man in society: all men were equal in the State of Nature because all men were the same. The Law of Nature, which implied the denial of the ever-varying "artificial" man of society, led thus to the single-patterned natural man, and the appearance of natural man resuscitated natural rights. Because since natural man was the ideal man all social distinctions between individuals were unjustified, and so the negation of individuality itself became in Rousseau an argument for natural rights. On the other hand, although the individual of the *philosophes* was an abstraction without the breath of life in him, all the same, individualism is along with utilitarianism one of the twin pillars of the age. Individualism begins the eighteenth century in the cautious hypotheses of Locke and ends it in the barren generalizations of Godwin. Mediaeval Europe at last disappears when individualism becomes the dominant faith; the climax eighteenth-century thought comes with the triumph individual rights; and so to the Revolution and n' teenth-century liberal Europe.

Taking the Revolution as an event in the histc thought we see, then, that it was by no means catastr It is generally admitted that it concludes and st the eighteenth century, but the fact is not always that this was at best but an interim summing historic process does not end here and anoth A superficial appearance to this effect is given ' forces that rose to the surface in the transiti' delusions of their extremest followers, are now become prototypes of the weapons of the armed and errant democracy of new Europe—which, if itself be principal victim of its own antique blunderbusses, need have small cause for wonder. What is wrong with European thought as a whole is that it has just attained to the phase certain thinkers achieved in the eighteenth century and finds that repentant and purgative beyond its liking. Those sceptics challenged the established order. Where are your firm foundations, they asked, on which you have builded your city? Their question has at last been heard and no answer found.

Yet for all that they were destroyers it was given to them to accomplish a work of emancipation such as few ages have witnessed. In a sense they are the true humanists of modern times. Man was their interest, and they must not be judged too harshly if along with the lumber of the ages they also cast out some things that are essential to man. They carried on the work—begun by the Renaissance—of emancipating man from the tyranny of old institutions: they asserted the right of the human spirit to its free self-development. They ploughed and scarified the fields and the little creatures of the field fled and the green grass and pleasant weeds were uprooted and there was nothing but an earthy wilderness; and when they sowed their seed it was sterile. But the fields were cleaner and purer that other men might come with other seed. In their own generation the harvest was small. Nevertheless, themselves enslaved, they fought for the cause of the free spirit and therefore their name is not without glory.

"Thankfully", writes Novalis in a passage the whole of which demands quotation, "Thankfully do we stretch out our hands to these men of letters and *philosophes*;

for this illusion had to be exhausted, so that true science might gain her rightful place. Poetry arises, like a leafy India, the more beauteous and many-hued because of the contrast with the icy, dead Spitzbergen of that armchair philosophy. To produce a glorious, luxurious India requires vast expanses of cold, motionless sea, barren cliffs, the starry heavens veiled by mist, long nights, and frozen Poles. The deep meaning of the laws of mechanism lay heavy on those anchorites in the deserts of the understanding; the charm of the first glance into it overpowered them; the old avenged itself on them; to the first breath of that new ideal they sacrificed all the world held fairest and holiest. Yet were the first to practice and preach the sacredness of Nature, the infinitude of Art, the independence of knowledge, the all-presence of the spirit of History; and so doing ended a spectre dynasty more potent and terrific than perhaps even they themselves knew".(5)

NOTES

I   1. Locke: Essay on the Human Understanding, I. i. 7.
    2. Id. II. i. 2.
    3. La Mettrie: Man a Machine, Eng. trans. 1750.
    4. Voltaire: Dictionnaire philosophique, art. "Chaîne des Êtres créées."
    5. See note 3.
    6. Dict. phil., art. "âme".
    7. Essay on the Human Understanding, IV. xii. 10–12.

II   1. Voltaire: Oeuvres, 1792. Vol. 46, p. 315.
    2. Locke: Some Thoughts concerning Education, sec. 190.
    3. Essay on the Human Understanding, II. xx. 2.
    4. Hume: Treatise on Human Nature, II. i. 7.
    5. Novalis: Schriften.

CHAPTER II

EDMUND BURKE
AND THE HERITAGE OF LOCKE

I

THE INCONSISTENCY OF BURKE

WITH THE BRIEF ANALYSIS in the previous
chapter to serve as an introduction to the system of
thought that prevailed in the eighteenth century, we may
turn to its more specifically political thinking. This, till
the generation before the Revolution, was practically a
monopoly of England, since the topic was too dangerous
for Continental writers, who, with the notable exception
of Montesquieu, were generally compelled to cut the
Gordian knot of constitutional questions by supporting
benevolent despotism. On the other hand, the two
greatest figures in the history of English political thought
stand the one at the beginning and the other at the end
of this age. Locke's ideas on politics are too familiar
to require summarizing when our object is only to
study the ideas of the eighteenth century in so far as
is necessary to appreciate the revolt against them. Moreover, because he was concerned with the concrete problem presented by the despotism of James II and with the
justification of the Glorious Revolution, many possible
developments of the English constitution remained
hidden from Locke, while many implications of his own
theories he left to be worked out by others; and of
these the greatest was Edmund Burke. In a sense Burke

represents the culmination of Lockian political theory; he is also the leading figure in the revolt against eighteenth-century politics, for although, in some respects, Hume had anticipated him, both in quality and quantity his political thinking is so much incomparably greater than Hume's that our study of the revolt must necessarily begin with Burke. For these reasons the most convenient procedure will be to take the theories of Locke and Burke in conjunction, to show how in the latter thinker the phrases and ideas of Locke are developed and interpreted until they are made to fit into an entirely different system of political ideas.

Burke has held rather a dubious position in the history of political thought. A political philosopher who is also a practical politician is apt to be regarded as somewhat of an anomaly and to be treated accordingly by other politicians during his life and by philosophers after his death. Of Burke we may say that had he been less of a theorist he would have met with higher rewards in his Parliamentary career, while had he been a less violent partisan his political ideas might have been granted a juster appreciation by those who studied them in the subsequent century. So intermingled with advocacy of party policy is his exposition of political principles, that those who set out to treat him as a theorist in the light of pure reason have generally ended by applauding or denouncing him as a politician in the light of latter-day politics. Mostly it has been applause, but of rather a self-regarding nature. In a political way of speaking, all things to all men, to Liberals such as Morley, Burke has seemed a Gladstonian who went wrong towards the end of his days; while to Conservatives like Lord Hugh Cecil the vision has been revealed of the great Whig as spiritually one with Disraeli and Young England. It is obvious that any account of Burke's theories which begins with assumptions of this nature is unlikely to give an unbiased view, though the temptation to label him in some such way is great, for even his own contemporaries did not know quite what to make of him. At the outset of his career he was fortunate enough to find a party ready to his hand for the shaping: towards the end of his life he drifted outside existing party categories altogether. Whigs and Tories, Liberals and Conservatives went on in their own way, leaving him to plough his lonely and despised furrow, which in later years both parties were proud to look back upon as their own. But there is only one school of politics for which Burke can legitimately be claimed, and that is the school of Burke. Any attempt to express his native thought in the shibboleths of an alien tongue is foredoomed to failure.

Another source of error, which has misled many students of Burke, is treatment by subjects. By taking separately his response to such events as, for instance, the American War of Independence and the French Revolution, the Wilkes affair and the agitation for Parliamentary Reform, his thought can be split artificially into watertight compartments, which can then be shown to be inconsistent with one another with the greatest of ease. This method establishes the very contradiction that it subsequently proves. Burke is no more immune from the charge of inconsistency than any other great thinker, but it is not to be discovered by taking in unnatural separation his ideas at different times. If he had been a man whose mind changed and developed in essentials as he came into contact with new experiences it would be different. But recently published material (1) demon-

strates clearly how little in after years he added to or
changed the stock of fundamental ideas he had garnered
as an undergraduate. And we must remember that his
mind, when he first enters English politics and his political
ideas first become of interest to us, was already mature—
details of policy not necessarily worked out nor principles
precisely stated—but all the elements present at the end
substantially there in the beginning. Morley established
once and for all the consistency of Burke in that sense.
But in another sense it is a very different story. Burke is
the greatest of the followers of Locke; he it was who filled
in the somewhat sketchy outlines of the *Treatise on
Government* and worked out the theoretical elaboration
which explained, justified, or condemned the many
expedients which practical politicians had devised in
putting the principles of 1688 into operation. But Burke
also it was who, not only in the *Reflections* but long before
the French Revolution, wrote of the political relation in
language Locke would never have dreamed of using. It
is not true that Burke changed his opinions fundamentally
at the time of the Revolution or at any other time, but it
is true that an inconsistency runs right through his
thought. The extent of his divergence from Locke will be
made clear if we take for study in the first place just those
aspects in which Burke might be assumed to follow him.

II

NATURAL LAW AND SOCIAL CONTRACT IN LOCKE AND BURKE

What, we will ask, has Burke to say about the fundamental principles which the famous Second Treatise
40

lays down? Does he simply accept them on the authority of Locke, or does he attempt to work out a fresh theoretical basis for himself? As he nowhere devotes a work specifically to questions of theory, it has sometimes been assumed that the former alternative is the true one. But if he does not ever definitely set out to treat of theoretical issues, Burke is all the time being brought up against them and compelled, willingly or unwillingly, to offer some answer; and the incidental discussions and *obiter dicta* resulting are often more valuable than a set treatise would have proved. For whatever he himself may say and believe as to his undeviating allegiance to Locke, actually he diverges in some most significant respects from his teacher. Let us take these fundamental principles in turn.

The basic political conception of Locke was that embodied in the theory of the Social Contract, which, of course, was introduced primarily for the purpose of making possible the transition from a state of nature to the social state. Now the object according to Locke of this transition was the inauguration of the rule of law— a conception to which the *Second Treatise on Government* continually appeals, and which is perhaps the political principle nearest the heart of England. When FitzJames Stephen declares that by his reverence for the rule of law Burke is nearer to Montesquieu than to the English tradition, he forgets that before Montesquieu was Locke, from whom it is that Burke as well as Montesquieu derives this element in his theory; before Locke, indeed, were Coke and Hooker, with behind them the centuries-old traditions of feudal and common law.

But does Law mean quite the same to the later thinker as to Locke? Times change and words and phrases remain, but they bear more often than not a new meaning to a

new age. Locke and Burke appeal with equal constancy
to the ideal of law, but is it to the same law that they are
appealing? A comparison of the two soon shows that
Locke, who hardly ever refers to the judicial power of
the actual State, continually invokes the Law of Nature,
for the enforcement of which he regards political society
as formed, and clearly bases his most important arguments
on this conception; whereas Burke makes use of it but
rarely, and when he does talk of the Law of Nature seems
to have something different in his mind. To discuss fully
what the term meant to Locke would be to enter into
pathless wilds of controversy; it is evident, however,
that it was really a pseudo-philosophical conception, and
could be taken as equivalent to the "law of reason"—
though what that might mean in its turn beyond a law
of common sense it would be difficult to say. On the
other hand, the law of which Burke talks is not a rational-
ized law of nature but a supra-rational law of God—that
law "by which we are knit and connected in the eternal
frame of the universe, out of which we cannot stir".
In just the same way his Contract is not the prosaic Social
Contract of Locke, but "the great primeval contract of
eternal society, linking the lower with the higher natures,
connecting the visible and invisible world".

Burke's conception of law presents itself thus on a
much more exalted plane than Locke's, but when we
come to the actual application of the theory the reverse
is the case; for whereas Locke uses his law of nature
merely as a philosophical basis for the political principles
he is anxious to set up, Burke passes directly from divine
law to the positive laws of man. Although in the eternal
law Will and Reason coincide, because of the restless
will and impious passions of mankind, he argues, temporal

42

laws are necessary to preserve the same coincidence on earth. Just government, he echoes Locke, can never be at the disposition of individual will. Above it, Locke had claimed, are the precepts of natural law; Burke says, in different phraseology, because all power is from God, by the very fact of being thus delegated it should be exercised in accordance with divine law; that it is so exercised is his conclusion in most cases. Human laws being merely declaratory of God's in his opinion, the respect which to begin with he attributes to the Law of God is thus passed on to positive human laws; and so it naturally follows that when he thinks of the authority of law it is with reference generally to some definite code and law-courts. When he declared dramatically in the indictment of Hastings, "Let him fly where he will from law to law;—law (I thank God) meets him everywhere", Burke had in front of his mind not the ever-present and unchanging law of nature, but the innumerable local laws of human society. This dissolution of Locke's Law of Nature into two distinct but closely allied concepts— the law of God and the laws of men—very largely reverses its function. The law of God is perfect, but its contents cannot easily be specified; the laws of men have quite definite contents but are very far from perfect. By linking them together so ingeniously Burke is able to justify all the ordinances of the latter on the authority of the former. Thus the idea of Law which for Locke in the form of the Law of Nature had been a ground of revolution is transformed into an essentially conservative doctrine.

True, it can be said that Burke is absolutely impartial in his application of the idea of law, and that although he starts from divine obligation and not from natural right, a despotic constitution remains to him just what it had been to Locke, a contradiction in terms. The arguments that Locke had used against James II he is equally willing to turn against George III. Again, shameful as he considered the incidental tyrannies of Hastings's rule in India, the attempt to defend these by a claim of immunity from law, the attempt to erect arbitrary violence into a principle, he rightly accounts the impeached Governor-General's most heinous crime. But on whichever side it may chance to arise the principle of despotism is always the enemy. Locke had denounced the tyranny of a King —Burke places tyranny and unprovoked rebellion on an equality: he refuses to recognize either absolute monarchy or absolute democracy as a legitimate form of government. In his Revolution pamphlets he condemns the lawless tyranny of the mob; in his Indian speeches he passes judgment on the despotism of a ruler with equal severity. According to his lights he fought against lawlessness wherever he found it, whether in a king's treatment of a colony, a governor's oppression of a conquered country, great States lording it over small, or revolutionary mobs governing by caprice.

The important point to be noted, however, is that this admirable result, although comprising a most triumphant vindication of the rule of law, and impressing it as a constitutional maxim firmly on the British people, was not in the last resort based on the same theoretic foundations as Locke's equally famous protest against Stuart tyranny. This fact becomes clearer when we go behind the Law of Nature in search of Natural Rights, as—the idea of law being meaningless unless it is taken as defending some definite rights—we necessarily must. Locke, like Rousseau, bases his case on the natural and inalienable rights of man. Burke, on the other hand, refuses even to speculate on the subject of natural rights, reserving them in his theory only as a final recourse against despotism: when tyranny is intolerable, he says, half unwillingly admitting that here lies the ultimate appeal, men resort to the rights of nature.(1) He employed the appeal himself against the tyranny of Hastings, but rejected it when the French turned it against their monarchy; nevertheless there was no great difference in essentials.

We might go farther, indeed, and claim that there is a remarkable similarity between the two greatest of the disciples of Locke, the author of the *Contrat Social* and the author of the *Reflections*. They both start from Locke and retain many of his ideas when they are really incompatible with their less restricted views on the psychology of man. Their minds seem to have worked out a curiously similar mixture of logic and intuition, which, presented in a fine enthusiastic style, was read and misunderstood by everybody. Both were realists or naturalists in politics, both were in the forefront of the romantic movement, both prophets of the reborn spirit of mysticism. And Burke, like Rousseau, was, whether he wished it or not, inevitably forced back on natural rights and apriorism. He is constantly concerned with the rights of men and so of Man.

But just as Burke's rule of law is different from Locke's, so are his natural rights: in fact, it is only with very considerable qualifications that he can be said to belong to the natural right school of thought. He declares in orthodox fashion that natural rights are sacred, but adds that he puts little value on attempts to codify them. In saying that he makes a declaration of rights not very different in effect from the French, Janet is attributing to Burke exactly what he refused to do.(2) Unlike Locke and the revolutionists, the only catalogue of rights he will draw up is one of legal rights. Natural rights, he definitely states, are at the formation of society abrogated and replaced by civil rights, to which henceforth man is confined, because as soon as any restriction whatever is admitted on the abstract rights of man, society passes into the realm of expediency.(3) Burke's theory of the change is that political authority must be admitted to be an artificial derogation from the natural equality of man, but that it can be justified on grounds of utility; natural rights are at best abstract rights, the rights men can look for from government are their own advantages.(4) Hence political questions are related primarily not to natural rights or wrongs, nor even to truth and false-hood, but to the positive good and evil of actual men and women.

The whole of Burke's career is a commentary on that text. His first great political crusade exposed it clearly: his objection to the English Government's American policy was that it had been determined by considerations of rights instead of according to the actual circumstances. On the other hand, he rejected equally the abstract demands put forward by the extremists on the colonists' side. In marginal notes to Pownall's book on the colonies he remarks: "Whatever they (the colonists) claim under the laws of Nature has nothing to do with our positive constitution".(5) His criticism of Chatham, as later of the French Revolutionaries, was that he allowed himself to be governed too much by general maxims. For himself, as he boasted to the Sheriffs of Bristol, "I never ventured to put your solid interests on speculative grounds". To sum up, Burke is, in the broad sense and with far more consistency than Locke, a utilitarian.

The lesson of expediency is to be learnt from him in full measure. It is a truth never superfluous to enforce that the happiness and unhappiness of actual individuals forms the final criterion of government: wherefore he will allow no end to be good irrespective of the means of its accomplishment, nor on the other hand will he condemn any measure merely because it fails to achieve theoretical perfection. Some inconvenience is to be expected; all government, every human benefit, is founded on compromise, the greatest wisdom being to know how much of an evil to tolerate. A statesman's manual of such phrases might be culled from Burke, who was given no more than his due when Mackintosh called him "one of the greatest teachers of civil prudence". And he was all the greater because with him caution sprang not out of the pettiness, but out of the largeness of his sympathies and the reverence of his mind. In this utilitarian context and not as belonging to the natural rights tradition is to be interpreted such a saying as, "The rights of the people are everything, as they ought to be in the true and natural order of things".(6) Not a rhetorical flourish of his rash youth this, but a solemn reaffirmation towards the close of his career of the principle for which he had so long striven, and in support of which he calls to witness very Christianity—"a religion which so much hates oppression, that when the God whom we adore appeared in human form, he did not appear in a form of greatness and majesty, but in sympathy with the lowest of the people,— and thereby made it a firm and ruling principle, that their welfare was the object of all government".(7) *Salus populi suprema lex* is the working faith of Burke. "Shew me a government," he summed up his argument in words that echo Locke, "and I will shew a trust."

That this was no phrase-making can be proved by almost any episode in the career of Burke. Here is the inspiring idea of that crusade against the oppressors of India which he himself adjudged the crowning effort of his public service. He called on the country to fit itself for world-wide dominion by abandoning its old parochial limitations, or rather by expanding them to the utmost limits of Empire. England having come to rule in India a civilization that was old when Western Europe knew only wandering savages, Burke demanded that she should respect the time-honoured customs of this ancient people, and conserve its proper and well-established laws. One cannot help wondering whether suttee and child-marriage and other religious and social abuses came under the heading of the proper laws which it was necessary to conserve. But Burke's final appeal supplies the necessary corrective, for, above all, government is only just when it is exercised for the benefit of its subjects. "I have struggled", he writes to Dr. Laurence, when his life was drawing to an end, "with the great and the little on this point during the greater part of my active life; and I wish, after death, to have my defiance of the judgments of those who consider the dominion of the glorious empire given by an incomprehensible dispensation of the Divine Providence into our hands, as nothing more than an opportunity of gratifying, for the lowest of their purposes, the lowest of their passions".(8) It is his claim that government is an ethical activity, and by this he breaks away from the immoralism of the school—supreme in the Revolution as in the *ancien régime*—whose principle, whether derived from theoretical Machiavellianism or from practical expediency, was *raison d'état*. The true principles of politics, he writes, everywhere the same,

48

are those of morality enlarged; and the theory of political trusteeship he enunciated with reference to India is the highest exemplar of this. His insistence on the duties of rulers forms the necessary complement to the Whig system of aristocratic government, and for its adoption as an integral part of the Rockingham Whigs' programme the world owes a debt of gratitude to Burke. Both Liberals and Conservatives of a later age were inheritors in a greater or less degree of the noblest relic of his life's work.

Returning to the relations of Locke and Burke, we see thus that the system of natural rights which Locke had retained as the framework of his political theory is practically discarded by Burke, who lets a conscious and noble utilitarianism provide its own justification. Such were Burke's views on the ends of political society, and on its nature his views are equally in advance of Locke's. The contractual theory being an essential element in the Whig political scheme, Burke naturally accepted it unquestioningly, but once inside his mind it was to undergo a strange metamorphosis. Its function in Locke had been to effect the transformation of natural into civil rights, and so to bridge the gap between the state of nature and the political state; which it did by setting up with general consent a government to enact and enforce the necessary laws in the ways and for the purposes prescribed by the social contract. The government thus formed gave society its only element of unity. Thus Locke: "It is in their legislative, that the members of a commonwealth are united, and combined together into one coherent living body. This is the soul that gives form, life and unity to the commonwealth; from hence the several members have their mutual influence, sympathy, and connection: and therefore, when the legislative is

broken, or dissolved, dissolution and death follows."(9)
This rather poetic description, with its "living body"
and "life", tends to give an illusory appearance to the
doctrine. Burke's close-clipped summing-up is more
true to it. "The idea of a people", he says, "is the idea of
a corporation. It is wholly artificial."(10) It is identified
by him with the duly constituted estates of the realm,
with its classes and corporations. When, as in France,
a revolution overthrows these, the nation disappears
along with them. "Mere locality does not constitute a
body politic"; that is to be found in the throne, nobility,
clergy, magistracy, property, and corporations.(11) Hence,
after the Revolution, France goes where these go—into
exile, and all that remains in the territory France had
inhabited is a set of usurpers struggling amid a chaos
of isolated individuals. Paradoxical as the theory sounds,
it is not without its merits: because smaller bodies within
a State, as well as being obstacles to reform through their
vested interests, are also the strongest barriers against
the growth of despotism, whether of one man or of a
multitude. If you will not be ruled by the organized people
in their classes and corporations, the author of the
Reflections seems to say, then you will be ruled by the
unorganized people—the mob; until in reaction from
anarchy the despotism of one man is accepted as a lesser
evil. France, he accurately prophesied, was to know both
extremes.

We already see that whereas the social contract had
provided a basis of resistance for Locke, for Burke it is
inclined in the opposite direction and becomes a bulwark
of conservatism. For neither Locke nor Burke is the
contract a vague, abstract agreement, it is quite definitely
the constitution of the country; and both would agree

that without the consent of all parties to it no power on earth has the right to change the constitution. Locke's theory thus enshrines a profoundly conservative principle, but Burke goes one step farther. He omits altogether Locke's precautionary assertion that each separate generation and individual has to decide anew whether or not to accept the compact already in existence, to effect which a new formal engagement is strictly speaking necessary.(12) In fact, he takes what is really correct Lockian theory on the point and pretends that it is an invention of the Foxite Whigs, and one which he does not scruple to characterize as subversive of all political freedom and morality.(13) By assuming that the social contract is passed down from one generation to the next he completely transforms its function. What can be said of a theory that takes the existent working constitution of a country, regardless of historical contingency, careless of the fact that it may have been set up only the previous year by a revolutionary settlement to which many of the people were not consenting, and by identifying this with the social contract, immobilizes social progress? Yet this is scarcely an exaggeration of the effect of Burke's doctrine.

That in spite of this patent absurdity Burke never freed himself from the trammels of contractualism seems all the more remarkable when we remember that already Hume had elaborated a theory of the origins of society and government which placed political conservatism on a much sounder and more realistic basis. But Burke was never willing to throw over an old idea, and moreover the theory of the contract was the especial dogma of the Whig party. This, too, may be said in his defence, that the contractual theory of the State was undoubtedly the accepted one and must in the eighteenth century have appeared to be justified by the facts. Internationally, only the sovereign prince was recognized, internally only privileged classes and legally defined corporations. Certainly Burke's theory was based on the facts—the trouble was that the facts were changing. That golden age of privilege was coming to an end, and Burke himself, as we shall see, at the end of his life came to recognize the signs of its impending doom, and played no insignificant part in bringing to birth a new conception of the State.

Still, even without abandoning the contractual theory in so many words, he tacitly drops it when he regards every man as necessarily born into political obedience, and as becoming, when he grows to adult years, automatically a full member of the body politic and subject to all the ensuing obligations. The justification that Burke would have given, if the need for one had ever presented itself to him, would have been that he could not conceive of the individual as a moral and rational being apart from society, by which he is shaped and conditioned and endowed with moral personality. Not merely a particular code of morality, but his very conscience and sense of duty are bestowed on him by society. A humble respect for the dictates of the social conscience is the least he can offer in return; to refuse to accept his due position in society with all its implications would be to renounce obedience not merely to a particular code, but to all moral law and utterly to cast off the yoke of duty. What room is left in a society regulated on this principle for the individual liberty, the right of resistance, in a word, the atomism of Locke's political philosophy? The only possible conclusion is that Burke has outgrown Locke; he has finally destroyed the system of natural law and contract, not by denying it, but in the only way in which an idea of value should ever be destroyed, by absorbing such parts of it as are fitted to be carried on and reintegrating them into the fabric of a fresh construction.

III

ORDER AND LIBERTY

We have seen in the previous section that Burke, and along with him eighteenth-century England, pushed Locke's theories to conservative conclusions. But despite the oligarchy established in his name, there was no evading the fact that Locke was a theorist of revolution and a prophet of liberalism. When the test came in the time of George III and revived Toryism, the true followers of Locke returned to his principles and resurrected against the Hanoverian king the protest he had made against the Stuart; and at their head stood Burke, acting conservatively, as he truly claimed, in the fullest sense of the word. Admittedly the constitution had imperceptibly been changing under Walpole and the Pelhams. The Whigs who opposed George III were in no way innovators, nevertheless they were the critics of a king, and took up their stand on a revolutionary settlement less than a century old—some might say on an oligarchical usurpation of less than twenty years' standing. However, the anomaly in the Whig attitude was unacknowledged by themselves. By the time when Burke was entering politics the changes effected, or assumed to have been effected, in 1689 were no longer matters of controversy, least of all to the Whigs, whose very *raison d'être* was the preservation of the principles and still more of the distribution of power

53

set up in 1689. By the rules of law and order the revolutionary conclusions of Locke were entitled to allegiance. The result was that Whig principles were generally taken for granted. This, however, does not apply to Burke, always more conscious of ultimate issues than the mass of politicians, and almost the first problem that arises in a study of his political theory is to consider how he based what we can already see to be a thoroughly conservative political philosophy on a revolutionary settlement.

We cannot acquit him of disingenuousness in this connection. A proposed "Address to the King", written in 1777 when party passions were at a high pitch, vindicated the revolutionary nature of the proceedings of 1689 in no qualified terms. "The people at that time re-entered into their original rights; and it was not because a positive law authorized what was then done, but because the freedom and safety of the subject, the origin and cause of all laws, required a proceeding paramount and superior to them. At that ever-memorable and instructive period, the letter of the law was superseded in favour of the substance of liberty."(1) If he had confined himself to this unexceptionable view there would have been no difficulty as to the position Burke took up on this question. Unfortunately elsewhere, and particularly after the centenary celebrations of 1689 in France, he adopts a different tone, still proclaiming, of course, his loyalty to the principles of the English Revolution, but unwilling to approve equally of everything done at the time, and laying emphasis now on the theory that the Whigs were defending the constitution rather than on the regrettable fact that in effect they deposed a king. Passing over that aspect of the affair, he vigorously asserts that such changes as were made were made in a conservative direction, that it was a revolution prevented rather than one made, and concludes by professing to base his condemnation of 1789 on the very principles of 1689. The other leaders of the Whig party were for the most part in disagreement with him at the outset, but Burke was convinced that he rather than Fox had preserved the traditions of Locke; from the Frenchified doctrines of the new Whigs he appeals without fear to the honest English principles of the old Whiggism.

Obviously as he shirks the problem set by the Whig Revolution, he certainly upheld its practical results; and there is a stage in political struggles, however difficult to define or rare of occurrence, after which he, like every disciple of Locke, is prepared to admit the possibility of resistance being just; otherwise there could be no meaning in political freedom. To few men of his century was resistance more antipathetic than to Hume, yet even he acknowledged a right of resistance, because, as he puts it with typical clarity, it is absurd to grant the people a share in the supreme power without at the same time granting them a right to defend that share from encroachment.(2) For Burke, however, resistance is only justified when it means that "taking up of arms in defence of just rights", which, as he wrote with reference to the American War, is not revolution at all. Throughout the greater part of his life he was a pleader for oppressed peoples, and in three or four cases a defender of rebels. But though his Indian and American speeches are one continuous indictment of a government which drove its subjects to rebellion, that did not make the act itself any the more desirable in his eyes. His prejudice is always on the side of law and order. He calls good order "the foundation of all good things"; liberty is worthless except

55

in an orderly community, and at bottom it does not seem possible to him that the interests of order can clash with those of liberty. In the reconciliation of the two is to be found the explanation of his somewhat equivocal attitude towards the Whig revolution.

He begins with Locke's thesis that liberty for an individual consists in freedom from restraint or violent treatment by others, and that this is only to be attained by operation of a known law with definite sanctions and an impartial judge. Burke goes further: his argument is that both liberty and social life are necessary to man, in fact that real liberty can only exist in an organized community, and that to enable an aggregate of individuals to act as such they must be in a state of "habitual social discipline". Liberty, in other words, is freedom, but it is a social freedom secured by an "equality of restraint", a liberty to do those things which society considers desirable. That society has the duty of suppressing any undue interference with the individual by his neighbours is orthodox Lockian and liberal doctrine. Burke says that society has also another duty towards the individual, that of exerting its pressure to free him from the despotism of his own blind and brutal passions.(3) "Men are qualified for civil liberty in exact proportion to their disposition to put moral chains upon their own appetites."(4) If they are unable to exercise this restraint society must do it for them. In the words of a modern idealist, they must be "forced to be free". Shades of Locke and John Stuart Mill!

A further qualification of Locke's liberty was drawn in the theory of Burke as in the practice of the Whig oligarchy: it was a liberty without either equality or fraternity. Feudal class relations still were the order of the day. We have already seen that Burke takes away the natural rights of the abstract man and is in consequence left with only the positive constitutional rights of political man. In a semi-feudal society the result is that for the liberties of the people he reads class privileges. But put it in a different way and Burke's liberty becomes Plato's justice—the principle that secures to every member of the community his due rights in his due place. Liberty in the abstract is a meaningless term to him; what he is concerned to maintain are liberties, and thus when he is enquiring whether liberty exists in revolutionary France, the tests he puts are practical tests. He asks if there is legal security for life and property, free disposal of person, and unrestricted use of industry for all individuals; either protection in the enjoyment of hereditary estates, or else a fair compensation, and finally liberty to express without molestation unpopular opinions on public affairs.(5) The list may have its faults, but surely it is better that positive guarantees of this kind should be given than that the individual should be enfranchised with all the liberties of a citizen of the world in theory and enslaved to an autocratic revolutionary State in practice.

The trouble, then, about Burke's view was that, as things were, liberties were so arbitrarily and unequally divided that they were equivalent to privileges, and so in practice it tended to become merely a defence of the privileged classes. Nor, taking the permanence of the existing order for granted, did he look forward to any extension of privileges to the rest of the community. It was only natural that revolution for the purpose of altering the constitution should be barred out; but does he mean also to exclude any possibility of change by constitutional measures? Yet has Burke not won the reputation of a reforming statesman and given us in his speeches on the Economical Reform an elaborate justification of reform? When this is examined closely, however, it is seen to consist mainly in drawing limits. Equitable treatment of existing rights is the main consideration, nor does he safeguard himself by any denial of the possibility of prescribing in an abuse. Reform, he allows, should be timely, it should give the people what they rightly desire before interlopers and agitators have taken up the demand and modified it for the worse, but above all it should be temperate, should not attempt completeness. If an existing institution seems to answer any good end, whether such were its original object or not, we should regard it as framed for that end and reform it accordingly. Finally, change must not be incurred except when the existing evil is patently excessive, nor pushed farther than is imperative at the moment. "Even when I changed, it should be to preserve. I should be led to my remedy by a great grievance."(6)

Thus, to conclude, we see that Burke's principal interest in the Whig Revolution is as a final settlement, not as a precedent; there is a great deal more desire to preserve than to progress apparent here. Natural rights and the social contract being put on one side, perhaps stored up in some Lockian heaven, he is left with legal rights and the actual Constitution: these are his grand concern. The British Constitution is the solid foundation on which all his theorizing is built, and the ark of his adoration.

IV

BURKE AND THE EIGHTEENTH-CENTURY CONSTITUTION

Practically, then, Burke's version of Locke turns out to be merely a justification in theory of the methods of the Whig oligarchy; and without delaying too long over the not exhilarating spectacle of eighteenth-century politics it is worth while trying to discover from Burke's writings what kind of outlook on political life that involved. We shall then be able to estimate the eighteenth-century political system in England at its height and seen through the eyes of by far its greatest apologist.

It is necessary in the first place to disabuse our minds of all the democratic conceptions of to-day. Whatever Locke's own opinion, his followers in England were almost without exception believers in government by the landed aristocracy, and Burke with them. It is easy to understand why he was so persistently hostile to the only party that challenged this view—the poor "Bill of Rights people". They were theorists, basing everything on abstract rights, whereas Burke, holding that the Constitution was not made on any such abstract theories, believed that it could not be tested by them. The theory in his idea of it should be evolved out of constitutional facts and tested not by its correspondence with some abstract standard, but by the results on the happiness of the people. With some truth he insisted that the agitation for parliamentary reform was artificially excited, that the mass of the people were not interested in the subject, and that the reforms proposed—an extended franchise, vote by ballot, frequent elections—would probably only increase existing evils by raising the rapidly advancing expenses of a seat to a height that only the Crown could stand. While he admitted the Commons might not be free from corruption, compared with the constituencies it was immaculate; and he assumed that an increase in the number of voters necessarily meant an increase in the amount of corruption.

Despite the stand he took in the Wilkes case, he gives one the impression that if he had to see any change in the composition of the Commons he would prefer it to be by way of diminishing its democratic elements. One would not have supposed the Parliament of the eighteenth century to be unduly democratic, but the defender of freedom of election found it necessary to protest violently whenever he imagined he detected any trend in that direction. The pocket and rotten boroughs were, of course, immune from democratic taint, but in constituencies where the electorate numbered as many as several thousands it had to be carefully guarded against. Apparently an absurd superstition, out of this in the mind of Burke emerged a theory of representation which has won general acceptance and proves of increasing value as years go by. His principal idea was that though a member should be in close touch with the feelings of his constituents, he owed it both to their interests and to his own dignity not to sacrifice his individual judgment; in other words not to lower himself from the status of representative to that of delegate. Carefully as he should watch over the interests of the people, he must on no account slavishly follow their opinions, nor behave as if he were a "canvasser at a perpetual election". Burke claimed that he was "the first man who, on the hustings, at a popular election, rejected the authority of instructions from constituents; or who, in any place, has argued so fully against it".(1) It may be alleged that about the same time Wilkes was the first member to pledge himself to accept instructions. Neither claim is strictly speaking accurate, but the fact is the problem as such was only beginning to arise. The real value of Burke's stand against the insidious delegate theory was not to appear until the franchise had been democratized, when a theory of representation which was totally undemocratic proved to be one of the essential safeguards of democracy: the delegate theory has never seriously challenged it. As Acton says, "Mr. Burke legislated from the hustings". His election speeches are "an epoch in constitutional history".(2) But though these ideas on representation may not before this have been proclaimed openly and with vigour, they are none the less implicit in the traditional Whig system of aristocratic rule, and they enter Burke's theory as a corollary of his views on trusteeship.

It follows from Burke's representative theory that the member of Parliament, whilst not neglecting local interests, should never abandon the good of the whole for their sake. "Parliament is not a *congress* of ambassadors from different and hostile interests"; it is "a *deliberative* assembly of *one* nation, with *one* interest, that of the whole". Burke did not hesitate to suit his actions to his fine words. Towards his own constituents of Bristol he paid no more than what he called "decent attention". Others thinking he paid less than was decent, he lost the seat, though the main causes of the alienation of Bristol from him were his acknowledged Catholic sympathies and his honourable refusal to be a silent witness of the crushing of Irish trade.

At the same time he fully realized that election, by putting the force of public opinion behind some part of the members, formed the real source of the strength of Parliament, which could never, without disregard for its own interests, alienate its constituents. During the struggle with the King he grew almost lyrical in his exhortations to the Commons to incorporate themselves with the people, to bring in the people to redress the balance of the Constitution. Taxation of the colonies without direct representation of their inhabitants would, he thought, lead to catastrophe in America and establish a fatal precedent for the enslaving of England. Against those who said that they were virtually represented, he argued that it was absurd to suppose that a kind of representation that had proved insufficient for Wales and the Palatine counties should be satisfactory for a far greater and far more distant part of our territories.

At other times he shows a considerable predilection for this same dangerous doctrine of virtual representation. All he pleads for in Ireland, he writes in 1797, is that the representation shall be sympathetic, not chosen on a system directly hostile to the majority of the inhabitants. "Virtual representation is that in which there is a communion of interests, and a sympathy in feeling and desires, between those who act in the name of any description of people, and the people in whose name they act, though the trustees are not actually chosen by them. This is virtual representation. Such a representation I think to be, in many cases, even better than the actual. It possesses most of its advantages, and is free from many of its inconveniences; it corrects the irregularities in the literal representation, when the shifting current of human affairs, or the acting of public interests in different ways, carry it obliquely from its first line of direction. The people may err in their choice; but common interest and common sentiment are rarely mistaken. But this sort of virtual representation cannot have a long or sure existence, if it has not a substratum in the actual. The member must have some relation to the constituent."(3) Clearly this is a little difficult to reconcile with his American speeches; all the same the description of virtual representation as he gives it here would serve admirably as an account of his ideal system.

Burke's views on the relations that should hold between government and people plainly require further elucidation. Thoroughly feudal or even patriarchal in spirit, he holds that it is the duty of the people humbly to accept the guidance of their betters; if these "miserable sheep" desert their shepherds it is only to become the victims of one another's passions and the prey of impostors. When he wrote, "The tyranny of a multitude is but a multiplied tyranny", he was referring to conditions in revolutionary France, but his mind may well have turned back to the furious scenes London witnessed what time Lord George Gordon led the brawls, when he himself shouldered a musket in defence of a friend's house, while the government sent troops to defend his own. Such an experience would not inspire an ardent admiration of the qualities of the populace: in the *Annual Register* for 1781 he wrote that after this exhibition of "the fury of an enraged rabble" the harshest despotism seemed preferable. Nor was this an isolated instance; the London mob was often out during the course of the century, and when it was out all peaceable citizens kept in. Unlike the theorist who "loved humanity but hated people", Burke appreciated highly the merits of the ordinary man—indeed, his relations

63

with servants, dependents, and friends in humbler stations form one of the pleasantest chapters in his life—but not equally highly the political capacity of the common people. As early as 1776, when the London mob had been gained over by the Crown, he advised a friend to draw a lesson from "the unprincipled behaviour of a corrupt and licentious people; that is, never to sacrifice his principles to the hope of attaining their affections. . . . Put as little trust in them as in princes."(4) Two failings of public opinion which he singles out for especial mention are the inveterate religious prejudices of the people and the general eagerness for war. The mitigation of the hardships of the English Catholics and the stopping of the American War were, he alleges, both only rendered possible by the intervention of an independent Parliament.

As for the democratic theory that the prime aim of government is to express the will of the people, regardless of what that will may be, or by what process formed, ignoring the possibility that the people may not have a coherent opinion on each and all of the innumerable issues that statesmen are called on to decide, heedless that government is a matter of reason as well as of will— Burke never took it for a serious contribution to political thinking. Perhaps it would have been better for the prospects of democracy to-day if nineteenth-century politicians had shared some of his scepticism, but the idea of democracy is so straight-forward and apparently just that long experience is required before the difficulties of its practical operation are realized. What is really remarkable is that the principle of majority rule had a century earlier been stated as clearly as could be by Locke, who, in this respect as in many others, showed himself far more liberal than his followers. The will of the majority, Locke premised, is the strongest force in the community, and since unity of action is essential if the community is to continue to exist, the minority must bow to *force majeure*, "And thus every man, by consenting with others to make one body politic under one government, puts himself under an obligation, to every one of that society, to submit to the determination of the majority, and to be concluded by it; or else this original compact, whereby he with others incorporate into one society would signify nothing."(5) He puts the case with supreme common sense, but the unrealized assumptions concerning the nature of political man are appalling. Locke's service in laying down boldly on the morrow of the abdication of monarchy the principle of democracy is great. But, that having been done, it was needful to go back and retrace with greater deliberation and with a fuller consciousness of the issues involved the necessary steps in the evolution of democracy. To reckon Burke's position as a retrogression would be a mistake; his theories were part of the inevitable deepening and broadening which was bound to follow on the brilliant but superficial guess-work of Locke.

If Burke was doubtful of the divine inspiration of the voice of the people, however, he was not at all ignorant of the power of public opinion. When he says that all power originates from the people, he means, firstly, that society is constituted by common agreements, secondly that the interests of the people should be the prime aim of government, and thirdly that all authority is based on opinion. The democratic sentiments we find scattered about his works can nearly all be classified under one or other of these heads, though an understanding of the position he adopts is complicated by the fact that occa-

E

sionally he cannot help talking of the "will of the majority" or the "voice of the people" just as though he were a democrat himself. The explanation is that he uses these terms in an opposite sense and not as synonymous with the populace or the masses. By the people in a political sense he says he means those of adult age but not of declining faculties, with tolerable leisure and means of information, and above menial dependence—some 400,000 altogether. This body is the natural representative of the nation; it is the public. Moreover, we only obtain the true voice of the people when this public expresses its opinion with due deliberation through the channels constitutionally provided. In the end the constitutional arrangements of each country determine what Burke will accept as the will of the people. His real will of the people is a conception with the same fundamental object as Rousseau's general will; they are both dreaming of an ideally enlightened public opinion. But whereas his is a practical entity discoverable by practical tests, Rousseau's is a metaphysical construction. They are both, perhaps, equally liable to involve confusion and misinterpretation, but Burke's was intended to describe the actual condition of political life as he saw it, while Rousseau was presenting an ideal state.

Actually Burke's 400,000 was a distinct overestimate of the number of effective political citizens in the eighteenth century. While political liberty had been broadening down from precedent to precedent, the franchise had been growing more and more restricted. Many seats were in the private possession of a single individual, others were jointly at the disposal of a few local landowners, most could only be won by the payment of large bribes. In eighteenth-century Parliamentary ethic the proceedings by which the composition of the House of Commons was determined ranked as "legitimate influence", not as corruption. The result of an election was often determined by influence before a single vote had been polled, and the decision accepted by the defeated party. If Parliaments were representative of the opinions of the landed class, what mattered the means by which they were returned? In pamphlets written during the Lucas controversy in Dublin, before acquaintance with the world had enlarged his mind, Burke had treated political bribery severely. For instance, we learn that elections should be held "without Corruption or Threats, without Fear or Force, or—undue Influence".(6) "The Nation", he wrote, "in which bribery is encouraged, in which it is winked at, in which the laws have not amply provided against it, and where those laws are not executed with rigour, that Nation must unavoidably sink into absolute slavery."(7) Association with the Whig party machine, to use a not very anachronistic term, cannot but have dissipated such callow innocence. "We must know", he once confided to Parliament, "that the candidate, instead of trusting at his election to the testimony of his behaviour in Parliament, must bring the testimony of a large sum of money."(8) Those ringing denunciations of Crown corruption which have inspired succeeding generations with a love of electoral purity must have sounded very hollow to Burke's own listeners.

In 1784, however, a change came over English political life that gave more point to the attack. In the previous year Fox's East India Bill had roused against the ill-starred Coalition ministry a new and potent force, which threw the wealth of the Indies into the scale against the Whigs, provided "the means of buying general courts, and even whole parliaments in the gross", and returned Pitt to power with an impregnable majority. The lavishness with which Pitt's backers were prepared to spend money had shocked even John Robinson—Sheridan's Jack Robinson—the hardened Secretary of the Treasury, who had managed the elections of 1774 and 1780 for George III. Such at least is suggested by a note in his hand on the back of an early plan for the electoral campaign. He observes that Pitt and his friends had indulged in "a wild, wide calculation of the money wanted for seats, but which I always disapproved and thought very wrong".(9) If even Robinson was alarmed at the wholesale purchase of seats previously more or less immune from the charge of venality and the resultant overthrow of old and recognized influences, the fury of the Whigs can be imagined.

What is strange is that for a long time they did not realize that the election of 1784 had reduced their political system to an absurdity. The existing party system, in fact, was ended, and the rule of the Whig families overthrown. Although there is some evidence for Professor Holland Rose's view that the Court and the East India Company's directors managed in conjunction to stir up a considerable popular agitation, it is difficult to agree that there emerged from the ruins "a party which may be termed national". The adjective hardly describes adequately the combination of East India nominees with King's Friends and dissatisfied Whigs by which the younger Pitt's majority was made up. However, George III had "dished the Whigs" for good, had put them in a position of permanent and hopeless inferiority; once they had thoroughly grasped that fact the conversion of the party to Parliamentary Reform was inevitable. But

Burke even now persistently rejected the only solution that could prevent political annihilation. He refused to admit that the Constitution as he knew it had broken down, but had no scheme to amend matters. Against the Nabobs, against the new commercial magnates, after that clumsy frontal attack, the East India Bill, had miscarried, he was powerless and knew it. His only recourse was futile denunciation of the policy of Pitt and George III— a policy, he said, which was based on a corruption of Commons and constituencies so extreme as to confound the power of distributing place and pension with the idea of government itself. What then, it might be asked in reply, was the policy of Walpole and Newcastle?

After all, what does Burke's political theory, so far as we have followed it, amount to but a defence of government by influence? His conception of government is oligarchic, its basis class distinctions: that was only natural in a man of his period. All eighteenth-century politicians preached that government should be for the people, none except a few professed democrats believed it could be *by* the people. Apart from one or two exceptional men, political leaders were almost exclusively peers or close relations of noble families; while the greater part of the Commons were the nominees of the landed aristocracy. Burke does not at all disapprove of this state of affairs, since an aristocracy marked by virtue and wisdom seems to him the natural fount of authority, from which the people must be content to take its political opinions. This is why he was so bitter against Pitt for appealing from the Commons to the constituencies in 1784; in so far as Pitt did manage to rouse public opinion against the Fox–North coalition, by so much would his crime be the more heinous in Burke's eyes; it was the duty of the Commons to correct public opinion, not *vice versa*. It is natural, he says, for men, who mostly have "a sort of heavy, lumpish acquiescence in government", to be influenced by their superiors in position and wisdom. For this reason, impressing on Rockingham in 1775 the necessity of arousing public opinion against the American War, he wrote, "All direction of public humour and opinion must originate in a few. . . . I never yet knew an instance of any general temper in the nation that might not have been tolerably well traced to some particular persons."(10) He insisted that "the people are not answerable for their present supine acquiescence; indeed they are not. God and nature never made them to think or to act without guidance and discretion",(11) and this it is both the right and duty of the aristocracy to supply. An often quoted letter to the Duke of Richmond in 1772 describes in elaborate metaphor the relation that should subsist between the aristocracy and the rest of the country. "You people of great families and hereditary trusts and fortunes, are not like such as I am, who, whatever we may be, by the rapidity of our growth, and even by the fruit we bear, and flatter ourselves that, while we creep on the ground, we belly into melons that are exquisite for size and flavour, yet still are but annual plants, that perish with our season, and leave no sort of traces behind us. You, if you are what you ought to be, are in my eye the great oaks that shade a country, and perpetuate your benefits from generation to generation."(12).

Here is the central faith in his constitutional theory, the quintessence of Whiggism and the negation of democracy. The justification for the "Venetian oligarchy" Burke upheld is to be found in the practical politics of the day, in the rapidly increasing greatness and prosperity of Great Britain, in the comparative well-being and content of the people. But conditions in Western Europe were fast changing during the long reign of George III. Burke, alive to the political significance of the rise of the younger Pitt and the new moneyed aristocracy, did not grasp its larger implications, or realize that it meant an end not merely to the Parliamentary system but to the whole national polity he knew. As a school of statesmanship, Burke's constitutional theory remains of permanent value; as a working system it was dead almost before it was expounded.

NOTES

I   1. A. P. I. Samuels: Early Life, Writings and Correspondence of Burke, 1923.

II   1. Works. VI. 99 (1772).
2. Janet: Philosophie de la Révolution, 12 (1875).
3. Works. II. 332–3.
4. Id. 335.
5. T. Pownall: Administration of the Colonies, MS. note by Burke (Br. Mus.).
6. Works. VIII. 5.
7. Id. VII. 230.
8. Id. VIII. 492 (1796).
9. Locke: Second Treatise on Government, sec. 212.
10. Works. III. 82.
11. Id.
12. Locke, op. cit., 122.
13. Works. III. 45.

III   1. Works. V. 473.
2. Hume: Treatise on Human Nature. III. ii. 10.
3. Sel. Lett. 269: to Mons. Dupont, 1789.
4. Works. II. 555 (1791).
5. Sel. Lett. 270.
6. Works. II. 516 (Reflections).

IV 1. Works: III. 26 (Appeal).
    2. Acton: Letters to Mary Gladstone. 4 (1913).
    3. Works. III. 334–5 (1792).
    4. Sel. Lett. 213 (1776).
    5. Locke: Second Treatise, sec. 97.
    6. Samuels: Early Life, etc. 380.
    7. Id. 352.
    8. Works. VI. 137.
    9. W. T. Laprade: Parliamentary Papers of John Robinson, 106 (1922).
   10. Sel. Lett. 200 (to the Marquis of Rockingham, 1775).
   11. Id. 207 (to the Duke of Richmond, 1775).
   12. Id. 155 (to Richmond, 1772).

CHAPTER III

BURKE: BASIS OF POLITICAL THEORY

I

THEORY AND EXPERIENCE

THERE IS A DANGER LEST the practical political wisdom of Burke should lead us into forgetting to inquire how he answers the more fundamental questions of political theory. Many have taken his assertions of loyalty to Locke at their face value, but the previous chapter shows that whenever we come to fundamentals he betrays tendencies entirely opposed to those of his master. Law, social contract, natural right, obviously have a different meaning to Burke from that which they had been given by Locke. The problem we are faced with is whether, while admittedly discarding the ideas of Locke, Burke had himself any coherent scheme to take their place. That is, has he a different definition of the State? For the nature of political society or the State is the essential problem of the political theorist.

What we are asking is whether when he wrote of the State, Burke had in mind the ordinary contemporary view, which took it to be an arbitrary aggregate of individuals under one government. This clear-cut view fitted admirably into the logical systems of Locke and his followers; it even fitted some of the facts. It was an adequate working description of nations as they would appear to any student of international affairs in the age of Succession treaties and partitions; while in considering the internal affairs of States the same notions of artificiality prevailed. Attention was concentrated on institutions, contracts, forms and ceremonies, and tended to neglect custom, convention, and all things which lacked institutional expression. The result of putting the formal before the real was that the principles supporting existing institutions, the motives responsible for their action, were deduced analytically, without any appeal either on the one hand to history and to the sciences of man, which, it is true, were as yet non-existent, or on the other to an adequate philosophical system. A peculiarly barren logic was expected to fulfil the dual functions of social psychology and philosophy.

Such was the essential weakness of Locke's political method, and, as his natural rights theory gradually passed out of fashion, its place was taken by a utilitarianism vitiated from its outset in the brilliant superficialities of Helvétius by the same error. Locke and Bentham each provided the theoretic basis for great and urgent reforms, the one after, the other before the event. But their political thought is necessarily ephemeral, because they both developed their systems on the assumptions of the *a priori* psychology of the eighteenth century. As explanations of the phenomena of social life they were hopelessly inadequate; as bases for practical reform they were magnificent. Their schemes were provoked by and suited to periods of administrative reform. Locke explained to the Whigs what they had done in 1689 and why they had been right; Bentham told the Liberals and Radicals of the nineteenth century what they wished to do and why they, too, were right in their desires. Each theory being eminently suited to meet the interests of the classes possessing political and economic power, opposition was impossible, and each in its turn became the creed of the intelligently orthodox. But there is, if not an interregnum between Locke and Bentham, at least an incipient revolt, represented by Edmund Burke, whose vivid imagination was not to be confined in the rigid categories of Locke, or satisfied by the calculated benevolence of Helvétius's school. Our object in this chapter is to attempt to discover in what respects he breaks away from the prevailing attitude towards politics; and this may help us to approach the further question of his conception of the State.

Disciple of Locke and Whig politician though Burke was, the real man stands quite apart from the eighteenth century and the *philosophes*. A believer in antiquity in an age when the Moderns had definitely conquered in their struggle with the Ancients, an adherent of the past in an age that was beginning to look to the future, he was also a philosopher of unreason in the great age of Reason. It was an age that found a mysterious virtue and balm for doubting minds in abstractions and universals—above all in those grand abstractions called Laws of Nature, on which political thinking was still almost entirely based. Burke, on the other hand, denied altogether the validity of abstract, deductive thinking in politics. "Circumstances give every political principle its distinguishing colour", and he required to have a principle thus embodied, to be able to see the conduct that would flow from it, before he would judge of it. Procrustes, he said, should never provide his ideal of legislation. Universal dicta were never valid in morals or in politics, which were not matters for metaphysical argument but for practical working out. The professor might take a general view, but the statesman had to deal with circumstances, infinite in their variety, and he who could take the greatest number of circumstances in with one view would form the best judgment.

Let the practical man shun, therefore, the "crude unconnected truths" of the academist, and be guided only by a "moral and virtuous discretion".

There is, alas, more than a suspicion of insincerity in Burke's reiterated denunciation of theorists. Anyone who opposes him or who suggests any reform he dislikes can be disposed of without trouble by this means, since Parliament was not reluctant to listen to rhetoric about hard-headed business men—such as the honourable members themselves. It provides, too, the most inconsequent and random of great thinkers with a ready answer to the charge of lacking system or philosophic basis. Yet he does not maintain this position consistently. In his speech on the petition of the Unitarians, 1792, at the very moment when he rejects abstractions and universals as things by which no rational man ever governed himself, he is carefully safeguarding those abstract ideas known as political principles, without which, truly he says, all political reasonings would be a mere jumble of details. Elsewhere he has described the politician as the "philosopher in action". "I do not vilify theory and speculation", he exclaims in a tone of injured virtue, "no, because that would be to vilify reason itself. . . . Whenever speak against theory, I mean always a weak, erroneous, fallacious, unfounded theory." Theories, that is, are only to be regarded when they have stood the test of experience, or when they have been arrived at inductively from the facts and hence are not liable to the charge of abstractness. It is true that most eighteenth-century theory was grossly deductive, and that Burke did his best to introduce the inductive method into political thinking, but that scarcely justifies him in claiming, as in effect he does, a monopoly of wisdom. It is often said that his own political opinions

76

were rooted in theory, and, as we have seen, in so far as they were derived from Locke this is true. Of the rest, we might say that they are rooted in sentiment, in teleological assumption, in religious dogmas, and in an implied psychological basis. But these are not abstract ideas, they are facts for Burke. The difficulty was that as yet there existed none of the sciences of society, lacking which he had to fall back on his own empirical guess-work.

His great merit was that while the *philosophes* were still carrying on an arid natural-right politics, he was already pointing the way to a scientific study of man in society. Unlike the rest of his century, Burke went not to the logicians, but to the market-place for his psychology: he called it human nature. Difficult as it is for us to realize, this was a new discovery in the eighteenth century; one has only to read any typical work of the time dealing with individual or social psychology to appreciate the world of difference in Burke. He had lighted, by accident or genius, on "the ocean of being", to use Locke's expressive phrase. To understand human nature he hardly dared to aspire, but hoped to be able to recognize its reactions and thus find some guidance. Rejecting Natural Rights, in their place he puts the instinctive demands of human nature, which seem to him a far safer criterion. "Never, no never, did Nature say one thing and Wisdom another." He has put in a single sentence the kernel of the difference between him and his contemporaries. "Politics", he wrote, "ought to be adjusted, not to human reasonings, but to human nature; of which the reason is but a part, and by no means the greatest part." How meaningless the distinction would have seemed to most orthodox political thinkers of a century before and after him! To them the essence of human nature had seemed to be the rational faculty, conceived moreover in a rather narrowly intellectualist sense. If they are to be admired for upholding an ideal, they are to be condemned for taking that self-constructed ideal for the whole reality.

But Burke was not the first to raise his voice against the extravagance of rationalism. His predecessor in this, to whom he owes, one cannot but feel, almost as much as to Locke, is scarcely mentioned once in his works. David Hume, sceptic, suspected atheist and Tory, was not a man with whom Burke was likely to claim affiliations; but Hume it is, nevertheless, who in the first half of the eighteenth century introduces clearly those principles which were to emerge more definitely later in the theories of Burke and the Romantic movement. Locke had substituted empiricism for rationalism in philosophy, but he still treated ethics and politics as deductive sciences of the same nature as mathematics. Hume carries the attack on rationalism into these fields and enounces a naturalism which anticipates in many respects the subsequent return to nature of the Romantics. Burke, whether consciously or not, is following Hume when he warns us in as early a work as the sufficiently bad *Philosophical Enquiry* that "the influence of reason in producing our passions is nothing near so extensive as it is commonly believed". He goes farther and destroys the strict utilitarian position in advance when he shows that men's passions frequently override their interests. Nor does he disapprove of this, though the only explicit statement to be found is in the cryptic form, "Under the direction of reason, instinct is always in the right". If he will go to this extent as regards all men, where the masses of the people are concerned he thinks still less of the power of reason. Civil society could not subsist if we were all

78

philosophers. Since man is a creature of habit, the mass of the people inevitably live by prejudice and custom, and wherefore should they not, for are not customs "the Standing Wisdom of the country"?(1)

We have now come very near to the heart of Burke's revolt against the eighteenth-century theory of society. We have seen that he rejects the "abstract" theorizing of Locke and the Natural Rights school, and appeals from their *a priori* psychology to actual human nature. This is where the difficulty begins for him. How are we to judge social phenomena, to advise on policy, without some abstract criterion? How, for instance, are we to know what kind of political organization is most suited to any particular community? Burke can offer no attempt at a scientific answer, but he can appeal to what seems better to him than theory, to the facts. That a community and a constitution have grown up together is the surest proof of their being suited to one another. Thus the appeal to human nature becomes an appeal to the facts, in other words, an appeal to the past. Conscious of ignorance, hardly contemplating the possibility of creating eventually a scientific sociology, he bows before the irresistible. Man knows little, has little power: for him to take over the reins, to try to influence the destiny of the race, would be no less mad than impious. Put your trust in the past, says Burke; there is no higher sanction than Prescription, for it is a guarantee of the long continued approval of God and man.

Prescription, then, is for Burke the most solid rock on which mundane rights can be based; it gives a title having for its sanction the eternal order of things; it is the master and not the creature of positive law, it is the decree of nature, it is the law of God. Hume had stated the theory rather differently, but though Burke introduces a theological connotation, it is difficult not to suspect him of some debt to the earlier thinker. "Time and custom", wrote Hume, "give authority to all forms of government, and all successions of princes; and that power, which at first was founded only on injustice and violence, becomes in time legal and obligatory."(2) Burke, too, holds that prescription is the most solid title to property and to government and so the principal base on which States are founded. More closely than this he will not inquire into their origins: a sacred veil should be thrown over the beginnings of all government. Original rights and wrongs do not trouble him, possession is nine points of the law of prescription, and undisputed possession for a long period of years the best title he knows. In this way only, by inheritance from his fathers, does he wish to enjoy his rights as a British citizen; and his Whig predecessors of 1689, he says, desired to derive the rights they asserted from no other claim, for the English Constitution is a prescriptive one. On the same ground, to take another instance, he bases his defence of non-interference with religions that are in possession, as the Catholic, which, he protests, is penalized in England for following the principle most necessary to society—adherence to the establishments of our fathers. For the same reason in India we must respect the antiquity of Hindu religion and civilization. Burke has, in Morley's fine phrase, "a reasoned and philosophic veneration for all old and settled order, whether in the free Parliament of Great Britain, in the ancient absolutism of Versailles, in the secular pomp of Oudh and the inviolable sanctity of Benares, the holy city and the garden of God".

This does not justify those writers who have regarded

him simply as a passionate and blind worshipper of the existing order. Such was the interpretation of Burke that prevailed at the end of his career and developed later into the doctrine of legitimacy, but Burke must not be made responsible for the aberrations of continental reactionaries, or judged by the invective of his opponents. True, a hostile critic might be tempted to say that Burke's main use for the divine providence is as a bulwark against reform. "He censures God who quarrels with the imperfections of men." The reformer has no reply to such an argument, except to suggest that Burke, when it suits his convenience, does himself criticize most violently these same divinely ordained imperfections. Still, resignation is his natural role: at the very end of his life, when melancholia and despair had become the settled habit of his mind, he could still preach to himself patience under the blows of circumstance. "The schemes of God are inscrutable." We must not question them; ours to accept the ideas and institutions by God established. Call established ideas prejudices, if you will, "Prejudice renders a man's virtue his habit: and not a series of unconnected acts. Through just prejudice, his duty becomes part of his nature." But the adjective begs the question, and that is the ultimate conclusion of all this rhetoric. In practice, moreover, he tends to neglect the qualification of justness, and so by his reverence for prescription he is led, says Leslie Stephen, into "a doubtful alliance with the bigots and the cynics". People were very apt in the eighteenth century to say, "whatever is, is right", and Burke perhaps more than most. The same critic, however, sees "another and a far nobler meaning" of the doctrine of prescription, in which it becomes "but a legal phrase for that continuity of past and present, and that solidarity between all parts of the political order, the perception of which is the essential condition of sound political reasoning".(3)

A corollary of the theory of prescription is naturally a eulogy on the wisdom of antiquity. "Veneration for antiquity is congenial to the human mind." Burke began, he said, with a profound reverence for the wisdom of our forefathers, and a profound distrust of his own abilities. "We know that *we* have made no discoveries, and we think that no discoveries are to be made, in morality; nor many in the great principles of government, nor in the ideas of liberty, which were understood long before we were born, altogether as well as they will be after the grave has heaped its mould upon our presumption, and the silent tomb shall have imposed its law on our pert loquacity."(4) Adherence to its ancient and established maxims he deems the most necessary principle for a country that would conserve its freedom. As his fear and distaste for modern politics grows, his admiration for the past increases. At the beginning of the *Account of the European Settlements in America* he had spoken of the manners of the Middle Ages as "wholly barbarous"; in the *Reflections* he sadly looks back on the "generosity and dignity of thinking of the fourteenth century".

The conclusion Burke draws from all this is that attempts to improve on the past are dangerous, and any political events which stimulate inquiry or innovation to be lamented. The American Revolution, thus, he frankly confessed to have shaken the basis of many accepted opinions; and he continues, "I am much against any further experiments which tend to put to the proof any more of these allowed opinions, which contribute so much to public tranquillity". Similarly it formed his bitterest accusation against Warren Hastings that "he dared to make the wicked and flagitious experiment which I have stated, an experiment upon the happiness of a numerous people". That such experiments might succeed does not enter into his calculations. Could he not, appealing to many a melancholy precedent, have said that history is the true school of pessimism? A prudent self-interest as well as trust in Providence dictates "that we should follow events". *Non mihi res*. "To the Deity must be left the task of infinite perfection; while to us poor, weak, incapable mortals, there is no rule of conduct so safe as experience." Thus, finally, the authority of the past unites with his hostility to abstract theory to throw Burke back once for all on the criterion of experience, that of the individual and that of the race.

At heart a profound pessimist, the best he can say is that, "Those things which are not practicable, are not desirable. There is nothing in the world really beneficial, that does not lie within the reach of an informed understanding and a well-directed pursuit. There is nothing that God has judged good for us, that He has not given us the means to accomplish, both in the natural and the moral world. If we cry, like children, for the moon, like children, we must cry on."(5) Along with faith in the past goes its usual concomitant, lack of faith in the future. To some critics there has seemed a remarkable inconsistency in the contrast between Burke's trust in Providence and his overmastering pessimism. It is the commonest form of inconsistency in the world, but he can justify himself by recourse to the factor which shares with Providence the shaping of events. For him the operation of Providence may be beneficial and God be justified of all His works, but in man is the root of evil. If conservatism be, as it has been called, distrust in human nature, then

is Burke the arch-conservative. In his thought, ever
religious at bottom, man is a creature bearing the taint
of Original Sin—that frowardness, pride in self, and lust
after innovation that came into being with Lucifer, prime
father of Jacobins. Nor does his pessimism find expression only in the clouded and thundrous sunset of his
career. As Acton notes, "In his robust and hopeful prime
he was as much opposed to the theory of Progress as
when the glory of Europe was extinguished for ever".(6)
Whether we take this pervading scepticism, this disbelief
in human endeavour, as the greatest proof of his wisdom,
or whether, with Acton and with Maitland, we call it
"his intellectual vice", the dominance it wielded over his
mind cannot be doubted.

II

HISTORY AND RELIGION

Burke thus turns away from the intellectualist psychology of the *Aufklärung* and from the theory of progress
in part based on it, and we have already said that his
alternative is embodied in the word Prescription. What
he does—to trace in outline the path his thought takes—
is to rebel against the eighteenth-century assumption that
its two chief guides—the law of reason and the principle
of utility—are synonymous. He uncovers the latent
hostility between a theoretical rationalism and a practical
utilitarianism, and gives his voice in favour of the latter.
But his utilitarianism, when we come to examine it,
turns out to be in the main an acceptance of that which
has been proved useful, or at any rate workable, that is,

of things as they are. Reason and utility both abdicate before the achievements of the past. To sum up, reason is displaced by utility, and for utility Burke reads history. Acton calls him "the most historically minded of English statesmen",(1) but the great historian is a far from uncritical admirer. Describing a conversation with Morley, Acton writes: "I ended by telling him that I would have hanged Mr. Burke on the same gallows as Robespierre. Tableau."(2) Both men were liberals with a deep historic outlook; but Acton was primarily a liberal, in Burke the sense of the authority of history and the claims of the past was the stronger, "and that alone devoured all the rest of his principles, and made the first of Liberals the first of Conservatives".(3) Burke was historic, Acton thinks, "to the detriment of his reasoning power and of his moral sense. He looked for what ought to be in what is. Is that not essentially Anglican?"(4)

Thus stated, the argument is unfair to Burke, whose standpoint is clear and reasonable enough. Society, he assumes, has been divinely ordained and its working is subject to the immediate rule of Providence. True, men are froward creatures bearing the taint of Original Sin; but despite individual aberrations God's will must be done in the long run. The history of any particular individual or of any short course of years may give us no guidance as to that will, but it is irreligious to suggest that the whole historical evolution of the community could go counter to it. To God, working through the community, embodying His will in its customs, laws, and institutions, we can safely trust. Here, in this divine process, is the most awful witness to the truth that Burke knows how to invoke. "I attest", he cries in his last, despairing speech against Hastings, "I attest the retiring,

85

I attest the advancing generations, between which, as a link in the great chain of eternal order, we stand."(5)

Burke, the critic may suggest, is merely borrowing from the *philosophes* their conceptions of humanity and of a deistically ordered world and reading them in a historic sense; or, to go farther back, he is simply reproducing in a slightly different form the mediaeval philosophy of history. Acton rightly enough fastened on to the historic idea as, from his point of view, the dangerous aspect of Burke's theory. His criticism is based on his conviction that truth and the eternal order are revealed by religion, that they are not deduced from history but are rather the criteria by which history itself is judged. Burke, on the other hand, would say that truth is not an extra-mundane thing stored up in some philosophic or religious heaven, but is a vital principle ever at work in the life of mankind and only to be found by studying that life. Although by his emphasis on Providence Burke seems to align himself with those who believe in an external arbitrary control of human development, the actual working out of his ideas betrays that half his heart is with the idea of immanence and with the view that closely associates religion and history. Acton was right in seeing in Burke's theory a fundamental opposition to the Catholic system of thought.

However, whatever be the eternal order, Burke does not stop at that. Accepting in theory the idea of a universal court of appeal, the eternal order, he goes on to draw an analogy between the general order of the world and the life of each particular society; for the contract of each single State is "but a clause in the great primeval contract of eternal society". Hooker, Comte and Spencer have inklings of the same idea, but, as Vaughan says, it remains

86

Burke's most original contribution to political theory. At times he seems to appeal to the "general order of the world" to test whether a particular system is in "just correspondence"; more ordinarily he assumes the general order from his observations of one nation—a procedure of which the legitimacy would follow from Montesquieu's rule of law; although from partial evidence, it should be possible to obtain the whole truth.

To the nation, then, primarily he applies the historic idea, and so doing steps out of the eighteenth into the nineteenth century. The social contract in which the community was assumed to have originated is, as we have seen, tacitly dropped, and he concentrates on the community, however founded. "Society is indeed a contract . . . but the state ought not to be considered as nothing better than a partnership agreement in a trade of pepper and coffee, calico or tobacco, or some other such low concern, to be taken up for a little temporary interest, and to be dissolved by the fancy of the parties. It is to be looked on with other reverence; because it is not a partnership in things subservient only to the gross animal existence of a temporary and perishable nature. It is a partnership in all science; a partnership in all art; a partnership in every virtue and in all perfection. As the ends of such a partnership cannot be obtained in many generations, it becomes a partnership not only between those who are living, but between those who are living, those who are dead, and those who are to be born."(6) A nation is "an idea of continuity, which extends in time as well as in numbers and in space"; this community is our real country—no mere geographical term, but consisting in "the ancient order into which we are born". In this society "mind must conspire with mind until time produce their true union"; and out of such union comes the national constitution—"a deliberate election of ages and of generations". "It is a constitution made by what is ten thousand times better than choice, it is made by the peculiar circumstances, occasions, tempers, dispositions, and moral, civil, and social habitudes of the people, which disclose themselves only in a long space of time. It is a vestment, which accommodates itself to the body. Nor is prescription of government formed upon blind, unmeaning prejudices—for man is a most unwise and a most wise being. The individual is foolish; the multitude, for the moment, is foolish, when they act without deliberation; but the species is wise, and, when time is given to it, as a species it always acts right."(7) No word here of the foreseeing and guiding spirit of Providence, but that is the inner thought, and under such protection the community becomes a vast, imponderable, all-enveloping entity, compared with which men seem no more than the minute grains which make up wide stretching sands. Each man finds value and immortality only in the life of the whole. Were the State to be changed with every new fashion, as, he says scornfully, has been the practice in France since the Revolution, "men would become little better than the flies of a summer". "Individuals pass like shadows, but the commonwealth is fixed and stable." Burke spent his life on his knees before the great mystery of social life. He worships with all the emotion of a deeply religious nature a society which is the temple of the living God. A temple? No, it is instinct with life itself and throbbing with its rhythm, a cosmic harmony of myriad men, more wonderful than the Newtonian universe or the music of the spheres; a giant organism amongst whose leviathan bowels he fears to probe with murderous scalpel.

At last we have reached our object in this chapter—
Burke's idea of the State—and how different it is from the
mechanistic theory we find in Locke or Bentham! And
if, as we have seen above, he fears too ruthless inquiry
into the functioning of the State, how much more will he
condemn innovation in its constitution. His conception
of the State comes to reinforce the conservative ideas
derived from the principle of prescription. Is a country
carte blanche for the theorist to scribble his vain ideas on?
Rather, the future of the State being conditioned by its
past, is it the duty of the true patriot to busy himself in
improving with the aid of existing materials, not in
inventing fresh data out of his imagination. All the data
of political problems are given and the statesman must
work them out from necessitated premises to almost equally
necessitated conclusions. Obscurantism was the nemesis
attending Burke's mysticism as well as his scepticism.
He dared not look for the root of institutions, says F. D.
Maurice, for fear he might find they had no root at all:
it would be truer to say he had a religious awe of uncover-
ing the subterranean processes of nature, a fear of severing
the root in rash ignorance.

It would require little, we can see, for the historic
idea in Burke's mind to pass into the full organic theory
of society, and indeed the strength of his expressions has
led some critics to assume that it does. Locke, however,
retained an influence in this respect salutary over his
mind, and he never yielded to the temptation that was to
prove fatal to so many theorists in the following century.
For all his imperfections Locke performed one great and
permanent service to political theory: he taught once and
for all that the value and happiness of individual life is the
only safe criterion in politics, that expediency is to be

defined as "that which is good for the community, and good for every individual in it". If we may take acceptance or rejection of this principle—that values are the values for individuals and not for some individual-transcending absolute—as the test of an organic or non-organic theory, then Burke's will certainly fall under the second category. If the term "organic" is taken, as terms in political theory often are, in a vague general sense to express some undefined feeling, then it may cover Burke's as well as any other theory in the world. But he himself is perfectly clear on the point and employs this very argument. "Corporate bodies", he writes, "are immortal for the good of the members, but not for their punishment. Nations themselves are such corporations." He is even more explicit in the speech on Representation of 1782, in which he declares, "By *nature* there is no such thing as politic or corporate personality; all these ideas are mere fictions of law, they are creatures of voluntary institution; men as men are individuals, and nothing else". Later, when under the influence of the pessimism prevalent in the nineties, men were beginning to speak as if Great Britain were a dying organism, Burke fights against this spirit, asserting that analogies between bodies politic and natural are only used to provide apologies for despair. In the *Regicide Peace* he explains that if he has used the term organism it has only been as a simple analogy. Commonwealths are not physical but "moral essences", he adds, and are in no way subject to physical laws of growth and decay.(8)

At the same time it must be noted that Burke's theory does not at all imply the doctrine of progress. Change he recognized as inevitable, since "nothing in progress can rest on its original plan". A gradual adaptation of ourselves and our institutions to changing circumstances is, in fact, the only method of preservation: the most we can do is to ensure that changes shall be operated by insensible degrees. Whenever any immediate reforms are under consideration Burke is apt to take up an equivocal attitude, but Vaughan, as he is wrong in calling Burke's theory in the strict sense of the word organic, is equally wrong in denying him any appreciation of the principle of growth.(9) As we have said, he realized the inevitability of alteration, and the only form he approved was that which can best be described by the very word growth; a slow change, analogous in its gradualness and unconsciousness to the processes of vegetable nature, or better still to the mutations and conservation of heredity—the latter an idea which Burke definitely imports into politics as providing a safe principle of conservation while leaving scope for improvement. Philosophy since the beginning of the century had been coming under the influence of Leibnitz's principle, only at the present day being challenged in the sciences, that Nature never makes jumps and nothing happens all at once. With Burke the idea penetrates to political thought, and in the next generation it came to dominate the historic school. The influence of scientific theories on political development has scarcely a better illustration.

Is Burke to be reckoned, then, a forerunner of the biologists, and his idea of the growth of the State placed alongside either Darwin's theory of evolution or else the Lamarckian theory? It hardly seems to us that the parallel either with the purposive evolution of the one or the natural selection of the other will hold. Of the two Burke is nearer to Darwin, for like Darwin's his evolution is not at all achieved of set purpose by the subject undergoing the process, but is an unconscious, unwilled growth. And again like Darwin's, Burke's theory is conservative in its implications. The difference between them lies in the side from which they approach evolution. Darwin takes it that organisms fit their environment because they have been adapted to it by evolving under its pressure, while Burke thinks they have been specially arranged thus by divine decree from the beginning, and so practically asserts a doctrine of final causes—noses were made to put spectacles on. The latter is as definitely a religious conception as the former is scientific. During the nineteenth century the idea of evolution passed from the one into the other category; present-day thought, to which neither seems an adequate explanation of the phenomena of life in itself, is still awaiting a theory which will take to itself and reconcile what is true in both.

Burke's conservatism, thus, is not, like that of the more recent period, scientific in origin. Neither is it philosophical: his Providence must not be confused with the Hegelian Absolute. Hegel, arguing that the only true development is that which follows the dialectical principle, permitted his philosophy to dictate what he alleged to be the course of history. Burke, on the contrary, said—what has been must have been ordained of God, and so gave precedence to the empirical element. His faith is something more than the ordinary philosophic idealism which believes in the existence behind the phenomenal world of a real world of noumena; Burke, like his friend Dr. Johnson, has no such doubts as to the reality of things sensual. He sees the divine plan in the actual appearances of the world, in the positive events of experience, and to him any system of politics that denies this faith is atheist, outcast. When Burke gives expression to the religious view of life it is in very striking terms, and the comparative infrequency of such references must not lead us to underestimate their importance. One would not expect to find it frequently on the lips of a political orator: affairs Parliamentary are seldom viewed *sub specie aeternitatis*; but a careful study of his opinions on practically any point will lead to the same implicit foundation. Nor is this strange. It is too often forgotten that the eighteenth century, rationalist and utilitarian though it might be, was also essentially the age of deism and the law of nature. Constant Biblical quotation had gone out of favour along with theological politics, but in no age has the deistic conception of a universe governed throughout by divine law held such sway over men's imaginations, nor, in that age, was any so possessed with the idea as Burke. Indeed, it was because it was so much a necessity of thought to him that only on very solemn occasions did he venture to invoke it in set terms.

Acton calls the religious element in Burke's nature his "catholicity", and Rémusat declares that Burke would have been more comfortable as a Catholic; but the suggestion is inherently misleading. The Catholic Church, the City of God, is the direct opposite and antagonist of the cities of this world; it can enter into no relation with them but that of mistress and servant. To Burke, on the other hand, the State itself has a religious sanction, the church is a national church not by accident but by its essential nature. His standpoint is even more than Anglican. One might almost compare his idea of the relations of church and State to that of those Greeks for whom the church was the State and the State the church. His ideal is neither Protestant Erastianism nor Catholic Theocracy; it is much more like the kingdom of God on earth.

The fundamental principle which emerges is Burke's vivid consciousness of the working of divine Providence in the affairs of the world. He assumes, to use his own words, "that the awful Author of our being is the Author of our place in the order of existence; and that having disposed and marshalled us by a divine tactic, not according to our will, but according to His, He has, in and by that disposition, virtually subjected us to act the part which belongs to the place assigned us".(10) However much he may seem to lose sight of it in the heat of party conflict and preoccupation with mere transitory phases of the political struggle, whatever emphasis he may lay on circumstance and expediency, at the back of his mind is ever present the conviction that an omnipotent Providence orders the mutations of human society according not to man's will but to its own inscrutable wisdom. There lies his first principle and there his final court of appeal. But if this is so, not even the community as it has been evolved during the slow lapse of centuries provides the ultimate foundation for Burke's political theory. From natural rights we are driven back to the rights of abstract reason; from rationalism to utility, that is to experience, and so from utilitarianism to history; from the history of the race to the history of the community; and finally we have to pass from history to religion.

If we go back to the Middle Ages, we find in the conception of Christendom as a unity although ruled by two powers, spiritual and temporal, some approach to Burke's outlook. In this way he anticipates the mediaevalism as well as much else in the Romantic movement. Theocracy and the divine right of kings, however, had both died for good, though the ghost of divine right walked abroad in the strange and untimely spectacle of

94

Legitimatism that began to stalk Europe during the Revolutionary aftermath. Burke's patronage has been claimed for this latter-day manifestation, but its principles and aims were quite alien from his own and in the *Reflections* he had condemned it in advance as nothing but an "absurd opinion". The enlightened despots had broken the necessary connection between divine right and conservatism; they had shown that monarchs might be as great innovators as anyone. Whereas Burke would submit all, the king as well as the humblest subject, to the same laws, moral and political, to which alone he attributed right divine.

By now we should be in a position to appreciate in its full bearing Burke's divergence from eighteenth-century tradition. The change is one of atmosphere and emphasis, of little immediate practical consequence, but sufficient to involve a re-orientation of the Lockian system so profound as to mark the beginning of an entirely new school of politics. The true spirit of Locke had passed across the Channel with Montesquieu, and found its proper disciples in the leaders of the revolt against Bourbon absolutism. Returning to England with Priestly and Bentham, it was to triumph in the form of utilitarianism over the abortive efforts of Coleridge and his friends to build up on the foundations laid by Burke an enlightened Toryism; one which trusted not in an *a priori* psychology, rationalist and individualist in the extreme, but in the empirical study of human nature, and which, while retaining what was good in the old, adapted itself to the needs of a new age. As a practical politician Burke had approved himself a true Revolution Whig in direct apostolic succession from Locke. He is a Whig with a difference, though. Locke's political philosophy is based on individual right; Burke begins at the other end with religious obligation. The great achievement of the former had been to free political thought from theological authority and bring it into the more reasonable realm of secularity and individual responsibility. The greatness of the latter lay in re-inspiring politics with a cosmic spirit and in teaching men again the deeper realities of social life.

NOTES

I 1. Mr. Burke's Table Talk, Mrs. Crewe: Misc. Philobiblion Soc. Vol. VII. p. 62.
 2. Hume: Treatise. III. ii. 10.
 3. Leslie Stephen: English Thought. II. 230–1 (1876).
 4. Works. II. 358 (Reflections).
 5. Id. II. 121 (Economical Reform).
 6. Acton MSS. 4967. Univ. Lib. Camb.

II 1. Acton MSS. 4967.
 2. Acton: Letters to Mary Gladstone. 187 (1913).
 3. Acton MSS. 4967.
 4. Id.
 5. Works. VIII. 439.
 6. Id. II. 368 (Reflections).
 7. Id. VI. 147.
 8. Id. VI. 145; V. 153.
 9. C. E. Vaughan: The Romantic Revolt. 131 (1907).
 10. Works. III. 79.

CHAPTER IV

BURKE AND THE ORIGINS OF THE THEORY OF NATIONALITY

I

BURKE AND NATIONALITY

THE TEST OF A THEORY lies in its application to the actual world and in this chapter it is proposed to put Burke's theories to this proof. If his theory of the State, which in appearance made so great an advance over contemporary views, shows no tendency in its application to the facts of the day other than to bolster up things as they were, then we may safely discount its novelty. Now no doubt Burke is at heart intensely conservative, but that is not necessarily equivalent to a mere supporting of things as they are. It all depends on what is to be conserved. As a Whig Burke desired the maintenance of an oligarchical system, which, because of its connection with certain political liberties and national achievements was not without merits, though it had equally conspicuous defects. As the founder of a new school of political theory, what he was determined to conserve was that "far nobler thing", the community cohering by virtue of a spiritual power. Nor was this a work of supererogation in the eighteenth century, when States were playthings at the mercy of their despots, to be enlarged or chopped up as suited the convenience of the gamblers who played the exciting game of international politics. Even in England national sentiment was languishing: the deprecatory and even discreditable sense in which the word "patriot-ism" was used is significant of the standards of national life. The fact is that except for a brief flamboyant out-burst under Chatham it had slumbered during the century. True, there was a certain amount of aggressive feeling, which was manifested in such episodes as the agitation which forced on the Jenkins' Ear War, or the violent anti-American feeling during the War of Independence, but of genuine nationalist sentiment little could be found under the first two Hanoverians.

That no one should have treated adequately its rise in England towards the end of the century may be because nationalism is generally regarded as having been indigen-ous here. It is true that England has been a nation and has possessed a tradition of patriotism since the Middle Ages, and the same might be claimed for France and Spain. Nevertheless, although nationality in these countries is a mediaeval heritage they share in the more specifically nationalist movement of the nineteenth century. Nation-ality as a theory is of comparatively recent origin. In Shaw's *Saint Joan*, the Bishop of Beauvais, discussing with Warwick the popular uprising in France under the Maid, says, "If I were to give it a name I should call it—nationalism". Mr. Shaw's bishop was right as to the fact, but nearly four centuries in advance of his age in putting it into words. It was not until the nineteenth century that men in general began "to call it nationalism", and under the guidance of such as Wordsworth and Mazzini to understand in some degree what they implied when they did so. The Revolutionary upheaval and the Napo-leonic dominion were necessary to rouse the nations to self-consciousness. But these events, though they may partially account for the age of nationality, do not altogether elucidate its origin. For its veritable beginnings we must look earlier. It is a significant fact in considering the causation of the nationalist movement that the first and possibly still the wisest of the theorists of nationality had developed his ideas years before the Revolution came on the scene.

Dr. Johnson had said that patriotism was the last refuge of a scoundrel; but to Burke, however it might be abused by ignoble use, the sentiment was natural and laudable. Passing over the fervid expressions of his undergraduate days, the speeches and writings of his maturer years are imbued with deep patriotic feeling towards his "second country". "We begin our public affections in our families. No cold relation is a zealous citizen. We pass on to our neighbourhoods, and our habitual provincial connections . . . so many little images of the great country in which the heart found something which it could fill."(1) "Next to the love of parents for their children", he said, "the strongest instinct both natural and moral which exists in man is the love of his country. . . . The natal soil has a sweetness in it beyond the harmony of verse."(2) This national feeling is the kind of emotional or instinctive desire which the eighteenth century utterly scorned. On the other hand it provides an excellent test of the sincerity of Burke's professions in appealing to instinct or nature against intellectualism; and it enables us to see to what extent his poetic description of the nation meant anything in practice. It explains, too, why the greatest of conservative statesman could be on occasion the apologist of revolution. That Burke should have defended revolutions must always seem a little surprising, but that he should be doing so at the very time when all Europe was ringing with his denunciations of the greatest of revolutions is quite astounding. Yet years after 1789 he is still able to turn aside from his crusade against the regicides to continue his indictment of Warren Hastings, and to defend, even to exult over, rebellion. "The subjects of this unfortunate prince", he declares, surveying the case of Cheit Sing, "did what we should have done; what all who love their country, who love their liberty, who love their laws, who love their property, who love their sovereign, would have done on such an occasion. . . . The whole country rose up in rebellion, and surely in justifiable rebellion."(3)

At least five separate rebellions against authority can be cited as meeting with Burke's specific approval—the Glorious Revolution of 1688, the American War of Independence, the struggle of the Corsicans for freedom, the attempt of the Poles to preserve their national independence, and the various revolts against the minions of Warren Hastings in India. There are certain features common to all these. Each was the rising of practically a whole community under the leadership of its governing classes in defence of what were claimed to be ancient liberties against violent innovation, and no approval of revolution in other circumstances should be read into them. Even so, if there is any general theory behind these instances, we are a long way on the road to a theory of national self-determination. It is proposed in this chapter to take in turn the various occasions which find Burke an upholder of national rights and examine his arguments on each case in detail. In the first place, the Revolution of 1688 must obviously be ruled out as not depending on the principle of nationality. Similarly, to take his championship of the cause of the American colonists as nationalistic would be profoundly to misinterpret his views. Far from suggesting that the colonists were entitled to recognition as a separate nation, his arguments were based on the inalienability of their rights as British citizens.

II

IRELAND

In this connection the case of Ireland presents a difficult problem, with which it will be as well to commence, as it is here that Burke's sincerity has been most directly challenged. Acton thought that Burke stopped short of conceding ever a full right of revolution, because of its necessary application to Ireland, to admit which would have ruined his career in English politics. "He could not speak out, for the system in Ireland was worse than the system in America. If there was a principle laid down against James II it was available against George III and his parliament."[1] Acton's argument implies that Burke recognized no system of rights that can override national liberty, but that, realizing the danger of these principles, he refrained from pushing them to their natural conclusions, more particularly in the case of Ireland.[2] The criticism, we must note, turns upon one particular practical issue and not upon the theory behind it, and in the particular instance Acton's interpretation is demonstrably wrong. True, Burke refrained from stirring up insurrection in Ireland, but as he himself said, that was on grounds of expediency, not of right. Keeping in view the circumstances of the time, he is hardly to be blamed for not daring to recommend the dubious arbitrament of war to a weak and divided people, even though he thus sacrificed theoretical consistency.

But, far from disregarding the wrongs of his native land, his Catholic affiliations, together with the Whig doctrines of toleration and the welfare of the people, joined the yet embryonic sentiment of national independence to make the emancipation of his Roman Catholic fellow-countrymen of Ireland one of the causes dearest to Burke's heart. He said in Parliament on one occasion that, "Nothing gave him so much satisfaction, when he was first honoured with a seat in that House, as that it might be in his power, some way or other, to be of service to the country that gave him birth; and he had always said to himself . . . (that if ever he were to deserve a great reward he would say) . . . do something for Ireland; do something for my country and I am over rewarded".(3)

What England could do for Ireland was of course well known. It was not that she should let Ireland set up as an independent nation: the demand in the middle of the eighteenth century was not for that, but for the granting of religious equality to the mass of the people. In the process of advocating this, a reforming, almost a revolutionary policy was developed by Burke out of essentially conservative principles. His constant endeavour was to prove, first, that emancipation could be granted to the Catholics with complete safety to the British connection, and secondly, that justice and interest alike demanded the concession. Rebellion, he asserted boldly, was not in the nature of the Irish; that of 1641, of which so much was made by Protestant zealots, had been grossly provoked; it was certainly not caused by the priests, who in any case at the present time preached loyalty to the King and obedience to the laws; if there was trouble in Ireland

the motive was not the demand for Popery, but the need
for enough potatoes to eat; the Pope in fact was politically
"as dead as the Pretender". All these opinions, which
he reiterates as late as 1795, were in a considerable degree
correct estimates when Burke wrote, though the follies
of Castle rule went far to change conditions in ensuing
years. That it was to the interest of the English Government to take advantage of favourable circumstances
while they lasted and solve the Irish problem by granting
moderate concessions he makes no question. Nor can the
historian do aught but regret the wilful obstinacy of
George III and the high Tories, which frustrated the
last hope of a peaceful settlement, exacerbated the dispute,
and prepared the stage for the dreary tragedy of nineteenth-century Ireland.

Of the justice as well as the expediency of relaxing the
laws against the Catholics he has no doubt. A constitution, he said, which shut out from all secure and valuable
property the bulk of the people, as did the penal laws in
Ireland, was "repugnant to the very principle of law".
"A law against the majority of the people is in substance
a law against the people itself; its extent determines its
invalidity." Are the Irish, he asks, to be reconciled to the
practical merits of the British constitution by being excluded from all its benefits? Finally, was the mere dog-
matic difference between Roman Catholics and Anglicans
worth making three millions of people slaves to secure
its public teaching? "I think he must be a strange man,"
says Burke, coming to that form of argument *ad hominem*
with which so often he clinches his case, "a strange
Christian, and a strange Englishman, who would not
rather see Ireland a free, flourishing, happy *Catholic*
country, though not *one* Protestant existed in it, than an

enslaved, beggared, insulted, degraded Catholic country, as it is, with some Protestants here and there scattered through it, for the purpose, not of instructing the people, but of rendering it miserable."(4) This language he holds in a letter of 1792 to his son. Even Burke would scarcely have dared to whisper such things in the hearing of the Protestant Commons of England; his public pronouncements on this subject are cautious compared with his private correspondence, though sprinkled with occasional outbursts.

His letters contain a masterly analysis of the Irish problem and proposals for its solution that were to remain unapplied for a century and a half. The Irish could not fairly complain of English oppression, he thought. If the Catholics as Catholics have a grievance, that is primarily against fellow-Irishmen. The only passion that ever influenced any English Government in his time with respect to Ireland, he says, has been to hear as little about it and to have as little to do with it as possible. The unhappy country has consequently been left at the mercy of a small Protestant faction, a "job ascendancy" which pretends that Ireland is perpetually on the point of revolt, in order that, for the merit of keeping down the rebellious Catholics, it may retain its jobs. All the evils of Ireland he attributes to the credit the English Government gives this cabal, and as long as it continues there is no hope of amendment. "No experience of the fatal effects of Jobbs will hinder Jobbers from Jobbing to the last." The matter is thus left in the hands of the Irish themselves and Burke has very practical advice to give them. He advises that they should make themselves as independent economically as possible; some century later the wisdom of such a policy was tardily recognized. In place of rebellion he puts forward a policy that amounts to passive resistance: "The resources of a persevering, dissatisfied obedience, are much greater than those of almost any force".(5) Again it was a century before the oppressed nationalities of the world learnt that lesson. Whether the Irish follow his advice or not, he has no doubt that emancipation will come to them sooner or later. "They *will* have it, because the nature of things *will* do it. What vexes me, is, that it will not be done in the best, the most gracious, the most conciliatory, and the most politic mode. In the present state of Europe, in which the state of these kingdoms is included, it is of infinite moment that matters of grace should emanate from the old sovereign authority."(6)

If it had been a question only of religious and economic considerations, however, the Irish problem would have had no place in this chapter; but they did not stand alone, and there was a further consideration which was decisive in Burke's mind. He saw that by the nineties the quarrel was no longer one between the people and a small faction among them, but between an alien Government and a whole nation. Yet Ireland as Ireland, he says, has no grievance against Great Britain. Constitutionally independent, politically she never can be so, being by the order of nature bound to the larger island. In a "Letter to the Free Citizens of Dublin", 1749, the young Burke has asserted that "absolute Independency would be fatal to this Kingdom".(7) She could only free herself of England to fall into the clutches of France: one or other must protect her, and for his part he offers no qualified allegiance to Great Britain—"my adopted, my dearer, and more comprehensive country".

One might almost call him an imperialist, though of a

type how many generations in advance of his day. His idea of an empire, as it appeared during the American controversy, was of a number of States under one head, monarchical or republican, but the subordinate members having local privileges and jurisdiction. He thinks Parliaments unfitted by their nature to exercise absolute dominion over distant States. Tyranny breeds tyranny. Rather we should admit the people of our colonies to "an interest in the constitution", thus binding America and Ireland to Great Britain and the British Constitution by the same ties of affectionate loyalty and honourable self-interest as were naturally operative over the hearts of Englishmen. The fact that this aim is a commonplace of modern politics must not prevent us from paying tribute to Burke's prescience in realizing such a possibility in an age when colonies were almost universally regarded as tributary states, to be used for its own advantage by the mother country while they were weak, but which would inevitably break away as soon as they were strong enough to stand alone.

Burke does not look on this disruption as inevitable, nor on the other hand does he wish to see the several parts of the empire united by too rigid a centralization of power. His great friend, Dr. Laurence, summarized his views admirably in a speech delivered in opposition to the Act of Union. Burke, he said, "had never had in contemplation any such measure as the present. On the contrary, it was his opinion, that the two countries had now grown up, under circumstances which did not admit of such an incorporation. But what he desired was, that the connection of the sister kingdoms should be reduced to a positive compact; . . . in which Ireland, with the entire and absolute power of local legislation, as far as she now enjoys it, should be bound on impartial questions of peace and war . . . to stand or fall with the fortunes of Great Britain."(8) Burke's position on the Irish question must by now be sufficiently clear. It represents not only nationalism, but a very enlightened nationalism at that, being in the latter capacity perhaps as far in advance of our time as in the former it was in advance of his own.

III

CORSICA AND POLAND

In Ireland, as in the American colonies and India, nationality was at this time only a side issue, but there are two instances in which we can study Burke's position on this question of nationality undisturbed by other considerations. Few striking outbursts of nationalist sentiment disturbed the complacent international immorality of the age until the Revolution and the Napoleonic Empire came to rouse the latent daemon of the nations. One tiny people there was, however, that waged in miniature a war as heroic as most ages have witnessed. The Corsican struggle for independence from Genoese rule aroused the sympathies of more in England than Burke, but Parliamentary references to the consequent subjection of the islanders by the French, who bought Corsica from its impotent lords, were inspired rather by jealousy of the increase of French power and loss of British prestige than by any nobler motive. In the *Present Discontents* Burke is content with condemning the English Government for its supineness, which indeed was generally criticized. He attacked North's policy because it allowed

Corsica to be subjugated and Poland partitioned "when by having a little of that busy spirit of intermeddling, both might have been prevented by mere force of negotiation".

References to international politics before the French Revolution are comparatively rare in Burke's acknowledged works, but some valuable material is to be found in the Historical Section of the *Annual Register*. The writing of this was taken on by Burke at its inception in 1749. Even if we did not know this to be so, many passages bear the mark of his pen unmistakably. In the *Annual Register*—and here lies the peculiar merit of this source—he allows his feelings full scope and writes without ulterior motive. We can trace his sympathies with Corsica and Poland through its pages.

Already in 1763 he had expressed the hope that the Corsicans would soon obtain their freedom, "which every people deserves to enjoy, who know its value so well as to risque everything to obtain it",(1) while on the cession of Corsica to France by the Genoese in 1768 he comments in striking phrase, "Thus was a nation disposed of without its consent, like the trees on an estate".(2) The incident seems to have shocked the public opinion of Europe, a fact in itself significant of a changing attitude. The account of the reception of Paoli, the Corsican leader, at Leghorn when he fled from his conquered island reminds us of the enthusiasm with which Victorian England was wont to greet Continental revolutionaries. The description in the *Annual Register* runs, "All the English ships in the harbour displayed their colours, and discharged their artillery, and though it rained excessively, immense crowds of people of all ranks ran down to the waterside to behold his landing and received him with the loudest acclamations".(3) Popular sentiment, though, could do nothing against *raison d'état*. Although France, by having previously negotiated a treaty of peace between Genoa and the Corsicans, seemed to have tacitly acknowledged the claim of the latter to be, as Burke puts it, "a distinct, and, in great measure, an independent people", the island was annexed ruthlessly. In 1769 he has to write the epitaph of Corsica as an independent nation: "All Europe were silent witnesses to the direct breach of a treaty to which the principal powers in it were parties; and to the ruin of a brave people, because they did not think themselves the property of their invaders".(4)

Another oppressed nationality claimed his attention soon after the extinction of Corsican hopes. Before 1768 Polish affairs are little mentioned in the *Annual Register*, save for an occasional animadversion on the constitution of that unhappy country, which seems formed, it says, "to give the most disadvantageous idea of liberty, by the extreme to which it is carried, and the injustice with which it is distributed".(5) Burke, who thus commenced with a prejudice against Poland, shared in addition the general Whig admiration for Catharine II, who had managed very successfully to combine despotic rule at home with winning the favour of liberal and opposition parties in Western Europe. The events of 1768 awakened his sympathies—ever at the service of the oppressed— for the Poles. "We have seen", he writes, "a foreign army, under colour of friendship, take possession of a country to which they did not even pretend a right; we have seen them, for a course of years, peremptorily dictate to the members of a once great and free nation, the measures they should pursue, and the laws they should establish for their own internal government. . . . It is not then

to be wondered at, that the Poles, a brave and haughty
nation, long nursed in independence, and whose nobles
had exercised in their respective districts an almost un-
limited sovereignty, should ill brook a submission to such
unnatural acts of foreign power.''(6) Despite the injustice of Russian policy, however, the follies and miseries
of the Poles seemed too excessive a price to pay even for
national independence. In the next *Annual Register* he
confesses that to become a province of her powerful
neighbour might be the happiest fate Poland could now
look for. "Can the wretched name of king, the empty title
of republic, or the ridiculous pageantry of a court, be
thought equivalent to the calamities to which the miserable
Poles are every day subject?" "Any submission to power
is better than so fatal and ineffectual a resistance."(7)

The lawless and brutal manner of the First Partition
arouses his indignation at the disregard exhibited by the
partitioning Powers for both laws of nations and rights of
individuals. With remarkable foresight he traces in
detail the ill consequences that will follow to them from
their unlawful gains, proving himself here as everywhere
the greatest of political prophets. Unfortunately, he adds,
they will not suffer alone, but in company with the peace
and public liberties of all Europe.(8) "The present
violent dismemberment and partition of Poland, without
the pretence of war, or even the colour of right, is to be
considered as the first very great breach in the modern
political system of Europe."(9) It is in this light, as an
act of peculiar international violence, that the fate of
Poland primarily affects him, as also, it is interesting to
remember, it had affected Rousseau. Even so his sentiments are striking when we remember that the lands
lopped off by the First Partition were mostly non-Polish,

and that true nationalist feeling was hardly manifested by the Poles themselves before the Second Partition. When that came, of course, Burke's attention was monopolized by French affairs, and though he viewed the attempted reform of the Polish constitution with a favourable eye, he declared that England was in no position to assist Poland. At the same time he maintained his opinion that, "No wise or honest man can approve of that partition, or can contemplate it without prognosticating great mischief from it to all countries at some future time".(10) "Poland", he had written to a Prussian gentleman as early as 1772, "was but a breakfast, and there are not many Polands to be found. Where will they dine? After all our love of tranquillity, and all expedients to preserve it, alas, poor Peace!"(11) The catastrophe cannot but have had in his mind a repercussion similar to that which Rémusat supposes from its impact on the mind of his whole generation. *"C'est peut-être au reste une indignation juste mais tardive, contre le partage de la Pologne, qui a le plus contribué à propager, et à accréditer en Europe l'argument tiré de la nationalité."* The oppressed nationalities of the world had, however, to wait for another generation and the dawn of a new epoch before the mind even of liberal Europe recognized their claim for what it really was. Burke's was, as yet, a voice calling in the wilderness.

IV

BURKE AND REVOLUTIONARY FRANCE

The critical stage in the growth of the idea of nationality came during the Revolutionary and Napoleonic period, and this at first sight may seem fatal to Burke's claims as a forerunner: because it was precisely in connection with the French Revolution that he demanded a foreign intervention that was treated by many as a denial of all rights of national freedom. That he should justify in the case of France what he had condemned unequivocally with reference to Corsica and Poland seems so very inconsistent as to demand further examination; but before we can understand the position he adopted with regard to the French Revolution a brief sketch of his general theory of international relations is necessary. Fortunately the *Annual Register* for 1772 provides us with a masterly summing up of the state of Europe and an exposition and criticism of the prevailing international system that can be by no hand but Burke's. Here the obverse of his nationalism appears in an idealized conception of the Commonwealth of Europe, as he calls it. Nothing could be more unjust, if reference is made to his international outlook, than Sorel's verdict that he was *"l'Anglais le plus fanatiquement insulaire des trois royaumes"*. He was intensely patriotic but none the less a good European, who, as he might have put it, could not have loved his country so much had he not loved humanity more. He would not have known how to separate love of his country from love of his kind.

Nationality, the only basis on which he was prepared to build internationalism, was to be reconciled with it by a very idealized version of European polity. "The idea of considering Europe as a vast commonwealth, of the several parts being distinct and separate, though politically and commercially united, of keeping them independent though unequal in power, and of preventing any one, by any means, from becoming too powerful for the rest, was great and liberal."(1) This is a picture rather of the ideal than of the actual, but in his later writings Burke is apt to speak as if the ideal commonwealth had really existed until the Jacobins shattered the bonds holding it together. For instance, he describes Europe as "virtually one great state having the same basis of general law, with some diversity of provincial custom and local attachments". That is simple nonsense, fortified though it may be by the authority of the jurists and philosophers of the century. It was a conception lingering from the Middle Ages, of no importance in practical politics until after the Revolution. Then, as Sorel has shown, the statesmen of the *ancien régime* turned to it to justify themselves and to make common cause against France.

Burke admits elsewhere that even as an ideal his notion of the commonwealth of Europe needs qualification. It does not, for instance, exclude war : that indeed is inevitable, it is for him the ultimate means of securing justice in the world, which nothing can banish. At the end of his life, when a call came, as he thought, in the name of justice, he answered it by preaching a holy war. But it is well to remember when reading his blood-thirsty philippics that the same man had defended nobly the cause of peace in India and Ireland and America. That he was no headstrong militarist is shown by the fact that he, like Rousseau, denounced as a perpetual menace to peace the newly developed system of large standing armies, which, because their upkeep exhausted the finances of the State, had to be given profitable employment, either in aggressive war, as in the campaigns of Frederick II, or, Burke would add, in the reduction of civil liberties, as in the American War. It should be added that actual hostilities in the field were only an intensification of the ordinary relation prevailing between eighteenth-century States, which among themselves were in a condition analogous to that of Hobbes's men in the state of nature. As the greatness of a State and the success of its ruler were determined by its power, and power was measured by territory and population, aggrandizement was the aim of every State. Frederick II, the most successful statesman of his generation, described the facts only too accurately when he wrote, *"Les princes sont les esclaves de leur moyens; l'intérêt de l'État leur sert de loi, et cette loi est inviolable"*. Burke, when he deals with concrete diplomatic transactions, does not disguise the rule of intrigue and self-interest. On the annexation of Dantzic by Prussia he comments, "There is not perhaps in history a more striking instance of the futility, if not of the absurdity of treaties, so far as they are considered as guarantees or acts of security, than the fate of Dantzick".(2) While such were the actual conditions of international intercourse, whatever idealists, lawyers and hypocritical politicians might say about the commonwealth of Europe, the fact was, as Mallet du Pan summed it up, *"Il n'y avait pas d'Europe"*.

The real working principle of the European system, as Burke recognized, was the Balance of Power, by means of which the self-interest of each particular nation was made the safeguard against general despotism. No doubt the system of the Balance of Power has secured that end, but he is not so wrong when he charges it with having been also the origin of innumerable and fruitless wars. "That political torture by which powers are to be enlarged or abridged, according to a standard, perhaps not very accurately imagined, ever has been, and it is to be feared will always continue a cause of infinite contention and

114

bloodshed."(3) Strictly speaking the culprit is here the principle of partition rather than the principle of the balance, but the one was an almost unavoidable corollary of the other so long as the balance theory remained uncorrected by any principle of nationality or non-intervention. Burke gropes dimly after some such corrective; but official recognition of the need and efficient response was not to come until Canning took charge of the Foreign Office and fluttered European chancelleries with proclamation of a non-interventionist policy.

Such was not for Burke. In the course of his analysis of the European situation in the *Annual Register* for 1772, he says: "It has been at all times the language of a voluptuous and frivolous age, that while a state is flourishing within itself, and suffers no immediate injury from others, it has no concern in the quarrels, interests, or misfortunes of its neighbours".(4) In contrast to this teaching he strongly asserts the right of a State to take an active part in the affairs of other States. The passage is interesting as it proves that when he came to uphold the same doctrine after 1789 his defence of it was no mere special pleading but was based on long-held convictions. "There is a Law of Neighbourhood", he writes in the *Regicide Peace*, "which does not leave a man perfectly master on his own ground; and as there is no judge recognized above independent states, the vicinage itself is the natural judge." This law might be called in effect the principle of intervention.

He lays it down explicitly and forcefully in a letter of August 18, 1792, offering his humble advice to Grenville. The passage is important enough to deserve quotation in full. "I perceive", he writes, "that much pains are taken by the Jacobins of England to propagate a notion, that one state has not a right to interfere according to its discretion in the interior affairs of another. This strange notion can only be supported by a confusion of ideas, and by not distinguishing the case of rebellion and sedition in a neighbouring country, and taking a part in the divisions of a country when they do prevail, and are actually formed. In the first case there is undoubtedly more difficulty than in the second, in which there is clearly no difficulty at all. To interfere in such dissensions requires great prudence and circumspection, and a serious attention to justice, and to the policy of one's own country, as well as to that of Europe. But an abstract principle of public law, forbidding such interference, is not supported by the reason of that law, nor by the authorities on the subject, nor by the practice of this kingdom, nor by that of any civilized nation in the world. This nation owes its laws and liberties, His Majesty owes the throne on which he sits, to the contrary principle. The several treaties of guarantee to the Protestant succession more than once reclaimed, affirm the principle of interference, which in a manner forms the basis of the public law in Europe. A more mischievous idea cannot exist, than that any degree of wickedness, violence, and oppression may prevail in a country, that the most abominable, murderous, and exterminating rebellions may rage in it, or the most atrocious and bloody tyranny may domineer, and that no neighbouring power can take cognizance of either, or afford succour to the miserable sufferers."(5) In contrast to this uncompromising statement, which moreover is in line with Burke's general opinions on the subject of intervention, we may put a rather disingenuous passage in his speech on the Quebec Government Bill, 1791. "If the French revolutionists were to mind their own affairs, and had shown no inclination to go abroad and to make proselytes in other countries, Mr. Burke declared, that neither he nor any other member of the House had any right to meddle with them."(6) Now, as he was convinced that such proselytizing was an essential part of the revolutionary creed the qualification was of little value. In any case, we cannot doubt that he asserted a right of intervention irrespective of whether propaganda had been engaged in or not. The letter to Grenville is very careful to make a distinction between two forms of intervention—stirring up dissension in another country, and taking part in a civil war already commenced—the object of which is clear. It enables him at the same time to condemn Jacobin propaganda in Great Britain and to advocate armed intervention by Great Britain in France.

It is only fair to point out that Burke did not, as some critics seem to imagine, invent all these doctrines *de novo* to justify the policy he desired to see put into operation: on the contrary he found them expressly laid down by the most authoritative of international jurists. Vattel, who published *Le Droit des Gens* in 1758, adopts a point of view intermediate between the Naturalists, for whom the Law of Nature was the effective foundation of international law, and the Positivists, who recognized no validity in international law beyond the systematization of the actual relations existing between States. This combination of natural right with expediency, expressed in an unusually lucid style, won great influence for the work and fitted it peculiarly to appeal to Burke. In an appendix to the *Policy of the Allies* he makes long extracts from Vattel, who provides for the case that had arisen in France thus: "If there is anywhere a nation of a *reckless and mischievous* disposition, always ready to *injure others*, . . .

it is not to be doubted, that all have a right to join *in order to repress, chastise, and put it ever after out of its power* to injure them".(7) Moreover when a civil war exists in a State, "foreign powers may assist that party which appears to them to have justice on their side".(8) This is precisely Burke's claim. The war, he says, is not against France, but a civil war within France in which we have sided with the monarchy. He quotes Vattel to the effect that if the "Body of the Nation" upon well-founded grievances depose the king, other States have no right to interfere. On the other hand, "In doubtful cases, *and when the Body of the Nation has not pronounced*, or HAS NOT PRONOUNCED FREELY, a Sovereign may naturally support and defend an ally."(9) The capitals show the importance he attributed to the qualification. He regards English interference in France as being sufficiently justified in international law by these references.

War is a terrible thing and Burke knew it. Historians who have treated him as a panic-mongering journalist, an arm-chair strategist, a war-fevered politician, must have read few of his writings. He thinks, of course, in the terms of his day: war can never be put an end to. But it is not to be entered on lightly. "The blood of man should never be shed but to redeem the blood of man. It is well shed for our family, for our friends, for our God, for our country, for our kind. The rest is vanity; the rest is crime." But even as a matter of expediency war seems to him desirable at this time, for dangerous as may be the enmity of revolutionary France, it is her friendship that he counts fatal. Most of all are the French to be feared when they come bearing their gifts of liberty, equality, and fraternity. England, he reflected gloomily, is an imitative country, and to him, as to most contemporary observers, the social systems of France and England seemed ominously alike. In 1791 he estimates that Jacobinism has more partisans in England than anywhere else out of France. They include most of the dissenters, "the whole race of half-bred speculators", the atheists, deists and Socinians, many of the "monied people" and "the East Indians almost to a man".(10) Most of his old enemies find themselves in the list! The danger he anticipates is not in the first instance from the mob; the greatest strength of Jacobinism comes from the fact that it has penetrated every class in some degree. He calculates in 1796 that a fifth of the political citizens were Jacobins. How exaggerated were these fears for England we know now.

Until the French Republic is crushed out of existence Burke declares that it will remain a standing menace to Europe. "The effect of *erroneous doctrines* may soon be done away with; but the example of *successful pillage* is of a nature more permanent"; there can be no compromise with a Power which has "made a schism with the whole universe". None is safe while a State founded on anarchy—a "strange, nameless, wild, enthusiastic thing"—exists in the very heart of Europe. We are warring not against a nation but against a principle: that, we may note incidentally, would be Burke's defence against the charge of allying himself with the enemies of nationality.

What was this principle called Jacobinism? Burke uses the term in a comprehensive manner, symbolizing by it all that is evil in the Revolution—and to him everything in the Revolution *is* evil. He consistently refuses to admit that there can be found the slightest justification for it, though it would be difficult to reconcile this attitude with the idea that was really at the root of his opposition to the American War. "*General* rebellions and revolts of a whole people", he wrote then, "never were *encouraged*, now or at any time. They are always provoked." In addition, the *Annual Register* for 1770, describing the struggle in France between the monarchy and the *parlements*, expresses sentiments strongly in favour of the latter. "How long this destructive power (of the King of France) may continue to desolate the country, or whether, as has frequently been the case, it may at length fall by its own enormous weight, must be left to time to disclose."(11) Shortly before, in the *Observations* of 1769, he had referred to the "injudicious" and "oppressive" methods of taxation in France.

At a later date he certainly does not agree that the monarchy fell by its own weight, nor even by an uprising of the people, since either explanation would make the stand he had taken difficult to reconcile with his own political principles. He falls back on the absurd expedient of assuming the Revolution to be the result of a conspiracy, writing, "I charge all these disorders, not on the mob, but on the Duke of Orleans, and Mirabeau, and Barnave, and Bailly, and Lameth, and La Fayette, and the rest of that faction, who, I conceive, spent immense sums of money, and used innumerable arts, to instigate the populace throughout France to the enormities they committed".(12) It is strange that he should have sought to account for such a vast upheaval as the French Revolution in such a superficial manner. He might have learnt better from his French prototype, Bossuet, who wrote, "*Il n'est pas arrivé de grand changement qui n'ait eu ses causes dans les siècles précédents*". Allowing for evolution of a kind, Burke's philosophy forgot to allow for that historical expression of evolution which we call revolution.

In addition to this fundamental error, he was persistently and almost ludicrously wrong in his detailed estimate of the state of French affairs. Many of his contemporaries were more enlightened and he tried laudably enough to obtain information about France. Doubtless his sources were not of the most impartial and his earlier visit had left him with a profound detestation of the reforming or philosophical faction. Naturally emotional, too, he allowed his sensibilities to run away with his judgment. In answer to Philip Francis, who in a shrewd criticism of the *Reflections* had called his sympathy for the Queen "pure foppery", he defends himself with betraying eloquence. "What!—are not high rank, great splendour of descent, great personal elegance and outward accomplishments, ingredients of moment in forming the interest we take in the misfortunes of men? . . . I tell you again,— that the recollection of the manner in which I saw the queen of France, in the year 1774, and the contrast . . . *did* draw tears from me and wetted my paper."(13) Moved by an impassioned pity in the first place, his mind only subsequently turned to the problem of rationalizing his emotions. In a sense the *Reflections* is one colossal essay in the art of special pleading.

Admitting, however, the inadequacy of his estimate of the origins of the movement and the irrationality of his motives, it still remains true that Burke grasped with surprising justness the spirit of those men who in the natural course were enabled to arrogate to themselves the leadership of the Revolution. Jacobinism, says its great opponent, is an attempt to eradicate all prejudices from the human mind, in order to put authority into the hands of men who assume themselves to be capable of enlightening the people. This involves the destruction of the whole ancient fabric of society, and the Jacobins bribe the poor to engage in this task by offering them as reward the spoil of the rich. There ensues a revolt against the established order of ideas and institutions, a revolt of the individual against the bonds and conventions with which for his own good he is surrounded by society.

This individualist revolt against society is the general theme of the *Reflections*; but Burke, struggling to understand a phenomenon almost beyond the comprehension of any man of the time, penetrates deeper and arrives at an apparently contradictory idea. Already in the *Reflections* he had remarked that the new democracy was falling under the control of a "base oligarchy". The process was destined not to end at that. "A military government is the only substitute for civil liberty," this was the principle he went on in predicting that France would fall under a new despotism, and it was laid down, not on the eve of the Empire, but long before, in 1777, and with reference to American policy. In the *Regicide Peace* he writes: "What now stands as government in France is struck out at a heat. . . . Individuality is left out of their scheme of government. The state is all in all. . . . The state has dominion and conquest for its sole objects; dominion over minds by proselytism, over bodies by arms."(14) Is this total reorientation of his criticism sheer inconsistency? Or does it reflect some change Burke thought he had observed in the character of the Revolution? He would have denied that any such change of principle had occurred. An inconsistency there is, but it lies in the revolutionary creed and practice, in the philosophy of Rousseau, not of Burke. He combines the two interpretations when he says that the revolutionaries had broken down all distinctions and reduced the people to a mass of undifferentiated individuals in order to gather them subsequently into a mob. Substantially that is a true description of the fate of France, if for mob you read army, as Burke himself did at the end of the *Reflections*. Anarchy and absolutism are apt to follow hard upon each other's heels and the French people have not always shown an aversion for extremes. In the practice of the Revolution, as in the theory of Rousseau, individualism and *étatisme* are inextricably mixed. It is to the credit of Burke that he perceived both aspects, though he had little doubt but that the absolutist principle would triumph in the end with the coming of a dictator. To the world at large, when history justified him, he seemed a marvellous prophet, and perhaps that was his true role. His accurate prediction of the course the Revolution would take is based on very little knowledge of the circumstances, and is a vindication of the virtue of just theory.

Burke's analysis of the nature of the Revolution seemed to him to provide ample reason for an invasion of France. The point he was careful to emphasize, though, was that this should not be construed as an attack on the French nation, because the revolutionary government was a usurpation. "We are at war against rebels, but the allies of the lawful government of France." "France is out of itself—the moral France is separated from the geographical." "At Coblenz only the king and nation of France are to be found." He never tired of repeating this doctrine, which seemed to him simple common sense and is to us glaring paradox. None of his opponents ever insisted more ruthlessly that the facts be made to fit a theory than here Burke. Theoretically he was entirely justified in assuming that the system of Rousseau was fatal to nationality as he understood the term. That is a point to which we must recur in our final chapter. In the meantime, every one knows that France after the Revolution was no less of a State and rather more of a nation than it had been under its ancient monarchical institutions. Burke erred because he would not face the fact that an important change might be taking place in political fundamentals; he only admitted the existence of a nation while it remained faithful to its privileged classes and historic constitution. Democracy was in his day still in the pre-Napoleonic stage, looking towards an ecumenical republic, and Burke is to be excused for failing to perceive that in face of common enemies it would yoke itself unequally with nationalism. How embarrassed and fleeting the alliance might become, our own times have shown but too plainly.

Although all the arguments with which Burke supported the war against France are not such as we should accept to-day, this is not to say that he was entirely without justification. The ground on which the enemies of the Revolution should have based their opposition was to be found in its international bearings rather than in its internal consequences. The Revolution was not merely against a government, it was against a social order, and one that was common to all Europe. Old Europe is not to be thought too wicked an animal for defending itself when attacked. The progress of revolutionary ideas, it may be said, should on the other hand have been welcomed by enlightened England; and if it had been purely a matter of the spread of French ideas, Burke might have deplored it but could not justly have opposed it by force of arms. That he would have been willing, even had this been his only justification, to join in the war against France cannot be doubted. But the spread of French ideas implied more, for it very quickly became bound up with the advance of French arms and the extension of French territory. A cosmopolitan pacificism may have suited the spirit of the *philosophes*, it did not satisfy the ambitions of French statesmen; and so it comes about that we see gradually emerging the shadow of Napoleonism. In this Burke will have to find his ultimate justification.

Granting that the Revolution was in its external relations from the beginning essentially an aggressive nationalist upheaval, in itself germinal of Napoleonic imperialism, and Burke is completely justified. If on the other hand, as Morley claimed, the French nation was driven to aggression in self-defence and thrown into the arms of Napoleon by foreign attacks, then Burke himself and his party were responsible for the appearance of the very evil they denounced. Controversy over this point began almost immediately and has continued ever since. Windham, who asserted that "the French Revolution did not need to be provoked to become mischievous . . . the aggressions were not the consequence of the resistance, but the resistance of the aggressions", believed that universal empire was from the beginning the aim of the revolutionaries, "the *primum mobile* that originally set it in motion, and has since guided and governed all its movements". This is an extreme view, but there are considerations which tend to some extent to substantiate it. Aggrandizement on the Italian and Rhine frontiers has always been the aim of French policy, and its abandonment in favour of the hated Austrian alliance must rank, along with Vergennes's pacific and Anglophile tendencies, as one of the secondary causes of the Revolution. True, when in the first stages of the Revolution Montmorin tried to gain support for the throne by provoking a war with England, the Assembly refused to follow him; but this frame of mind only continued so long as it seemed that a war would turn to the advantage of the royal party in France. That appearance of pacificism which won the sympathies of enlightened men all over Europe was for most of the revolutionaries only a by-product of party politics, though it also served the purpose of keeping England neutral in the critical first years of the Revolution. *"Mais il ne fallait point que la Révolution se mît à envahir, et surtout ces petits peuples que l'Angleterre tenait pour ses clients. Il ne fallait point davantage que la Révolution se fît provocante et sanglante: la sympathie de l'Europe éclairée, on dirait aujourd'hui de l'Europe libérale, était à ce prix."*(15) France was not prepared to pay it. If the early leaders of the Revolution were pacific, that was one of the causes of their fall before the bellicose ardour of Brissot and the Girondins.

With the accession to power of the Gironde conquest under the pretext of liberation became definitely part of the Revolutionary programme. *"L'intérêt national l'importera sur la raison pure, et non seulement il ramènera la France nouvelle aux 'guerres communes' d'autrefois, mais il l'entraînera jusqu'aux plus extraordinaires excès des 'guerres de magnificence'. Cette transformation s'annonce dès 1791."*(16). And we may draw the conclusion in the words of Burke: "The Revolution was made, not to make France free, but to make her formidable; not to make her a neighbour, but a mistress; not to make her more observant of laws, but to put her in a condition to impose them. To make France truly formidable it was necessary that France should be new-modelled." The national traditions of France dictated the policy which the revolutionary leaders followed, and the national traditions of England were not silent when Burke aroused his country to the reality of the French menace.

It is not as an "old Whig" or as a defender of property and religion that Burke finally appears in his crusade against the Revolution. That consciousness of the power of public opinion, which he always had, led him in time to the discovery of a new principle, and one to the neglect of which was largely due the failure of British policy. Time and again did Pitt and Grenville sacrifice opportunities through the rigidity and secrecy of their diplomacy. Talleyrand wrote in a despatch, "*Le ministère britannique est le plus secret de toute l'Europe*". So long as they neither could nor would make use of public opinion, they had to play the game of State with the dice heavily loaded against them. While the allied governments went on contriving ever new coalitions and military combinations, or else abandoned the struggle in despair, Burke by 1795 had become confirmed in his conviction that the republican spirit could be defeated only by another "of the same nature but informed with another principle and pointing to another end". In the *Regicide Peace* he brings all his powers of ridicule to bear against what he terms a "war of calculation"—surely an excellent description of the system of Pitt and Leopold II. He has been called enthusiast, madman? Well, he replies, the frenzy to which oppression drives wise men is preferable to the sobriety of fools. He can almost find it in his heart to admire the madness of the French rabble when he compares it to the sanity of "a league of princes against bad syllogisms".

In the field of propaganda as well as in the field of battle, he thought the best defensive policy was boldly to take the offensive within France itself by issuing a manifesto with a popular appeal. He says that it ought to turn "much more upon the benefit of the people; on good order, religion, morality, security, and property, than upon the rights of sovereigns. Previous to it, or along with it, ought to be published strong collections of cases and facts of the cruelties, persecutions, and desolations produced by this revolution, in a popular style; which, for being simple and popular, will not be the less eloquent and impressive. . . . Particulars make impressions. This may be cooked up a hundred different ways."(17) He realized that such a movement as Jacobinism had primarily to be fought on the ground of opinion. Writing in 1794, he says, "Opinion (never without its effect) has obtained a greater dominion over human affairs than ever it possessed; and which grows just in proportion as the implicit reverence for old institutions is found to decline".(18) We must not think that this realization of the power of opinion was a new discovery for Burke, who long before, despite his antipathy for the elder Pitt, had understood that the Great Commoner's power lay in his capacity for commanding popular enthusiasm. "He considered Mobs in the light of a raw material which might be manufactured to a proper stuff for their Happines(s) in the end."(19) But the natural leaders of the people should not degenerate into bidders at an auction of popularity, and to Burke, Chatham seemed to go so far as "to impair on some occasions the dignity of government".(20) Burke's career covers a period of extraordinarily rapid growth in public opinion, a growth which he recognized and reacted to, and of which his own writings were perhaps a secondary cause. The critic was before his death to impair *his* dignity and aloofness. Discouraged by the hostility ministers and Parliament displayed towards his views on the Revolution, he appealed over their heads to the people. One of the greatest of publicists, he had always

tacitly recognized that his speeches as well as his pamphlets found their real objective in public opinion. In the
Reflections he throws off all concealment. It is the manifesto of the Counter-Revolution and the greatest and
most influential political pamphlet ever written. Disregarded in Parliament, Burke had the nation behind him.
He it was, not Pitt, who rallied England against the
French menace: politicians might be blind, but Burke
knew, as the nation soon was to know, that it was about
to enter on a struggle to the death for very existence. If
it faltered or turned back that must be accounted to the
ineptitude of its governors, men, like the other rulers of
old Europe, ignorant of what a nation was until a nation
taught them. Burke needed no teaching: he knew intuitively,
and that knowledge is the key to his mind after 1789.

No impartial student of the Revolutionary War can
deny the force of Burke's criticism. Pitt was waging a
nineteenth-century war on eighteenth-century methods.
Burke, and for a long time Burke alone, comprehended
that a new system was needed. And the new force that
he would call in to aid, what was it but the force of
nationality? "To do anything without raising a Spirit
(I mean a National Spirit) with all the energy and much
of the conduct of a Party Spirit, I hold to be a thing absolutely impossible." No remedy there seems to him for
our evils but in that enthusiasm "which might create a
Soul under the ribs of Death". "New things in a new
world! I see no hope in the common tracks. If men are not
to be found who can be got to feel within them some
impulse,

quod nequeo monstrare, et sentio tantum,

and which makes them impatient of the present; if none

can be got to feel that private persons may sometimes assume that sort of magistracy which does not depend on the nomination of kings, or the election of the people, but as an inherent and self-existent power which both would recognize; I see nothing in the world to hope." With a prophecy on his lips of the force that was destined to set up and to overthrow Napoleon's empire, and with despair in his heart, his stormy career drew in sorrowful splendour to its close. "There is the hand of God in this business, and there is an end of the system of Europe, taking in laws, manners, religion, and politics, in which I delighted so much'. My poor son was called off in time— '*ne quid tale videret*'."

He died, but events moved on in the course he had foreseen. Gradually the Age of Dynasts passed away and was succeeded by the Age of Nationality, itself still troubling the world. He had no call to have lost faith, for the future was on his side; he had founded his theory of the State on bases too permanent to be shaken by a passing storm, bases the real strength of which only became apparent, indeed, in time of adversity. He saw, long before most of his contemporaries, the power and rights of that force of national sentiment which eighteenth-century theorists and politicians had conspired to ignore and trample on. The right of a subject nation to freedom just because it *was* a nation was a new idea in political thought. Though the fact had been there for centuries, Burke has the honour of first stating in definite form the theory of nationality. The remaining history of the Revolutionary and Napoleonic era is a triumphant vindication of the truth of his insight into the real sources of the strength of nations.

NOTES

I 1. Works. II. 467.
  2. Id. VIII. 141 (Impeachment of Hastings, May 30, 1794).
  3. Works. VIII. 39–40 (id. 1794).

II 1. Acton MSS. 4956. Cf. Letters to Mary Gladstone, 37, 182–3.
  2. Acton MSS. 4965.
  3. Parl. Hist. May 17, 1782.
  4. Sel. Lett. 345–6: 1792.
  5. R. Thierry: A Letter to Canning, 41 (1792).
  6. Sel. Lett. 323: 1792.
  7. Samuels, op. cit. 364.
  8. Parl. Hist. (1819). Vol. 24: Debate in Commons on Union with Ireland, Jan. 23, 1799.

III 1. Ann. Reg. 1763, Hist. Section, 49.
  2. Id. 1768. 2.
  3. Id. 1769. 44.
  4. Id. 1769. 10.
  5. Id. 1763. 45.
  6. Id. 1768. 4.
  7. Id. 1769. 6, 32.
  8. Id. 1772. 4.
  9. Id. 1772. 2.
  10. Works. III. 482 (Conduct of the Minority).
  11. Id. VIII. 455.

IV 1. Ann. Reg. 1772. 2.
  2. Id. 1772. 41.
  3. Id. 1760. 34.
  4. Id. 1772. 3.
  5. Sel. Lett. 351–2 (to Lord Grenville, Aug. 18, 1792).
  6. Speeches. IV. 13.
  7. Vattel: Le Droit des Gens, Bk. II. Ch. IV. sec. 53.
  8. Id. II. IV. 56.
  9. Id. II. XII. 196.

10. Works. III. 354 (1791).
11. Ann. Reg. 1770. 53.
12. Corr. III. 176 (1792).
13. Corr. III. 137–9 (1790).
14. Works. V. 255 (Regicide Peace).
15. Sorel: L'Europe et la Révolution Française. III. 142.
16. Id. II. 203.
17. Sel. Lett. 308–10 (to R. Burke, junior, Aug. 16, 1791).
18. Windham's Diary (1866), 322 (Burke to Windham, Oct. 13, 1794).
19. Table Talk, Mrs. Crewe. 13.
20. Ann. Reg. 1758. 11.

CHAPTER V

WORDSWORTH AND NATIONALITY

IT IS PERHAPS UNFAIR to blame Burke's contemporaries too harshly for their blindness to the growing force of nationality. The period was one of rapid transition, when some men were bound to be in advance of their time and some behind it. The age of Nationality was not yet born, and though it was evident that Europe was in sore travail it was not equally evident what would be the event. Pass to the next generation, and sympathy may be more difficult to give to those politicians who supposed in 1815 as in 1789 that things would go on in precisely the way that they always had within their memory: one can more readily make allowances for men who, finding themselves in unknown, uncharted country, deemed it better to proceed on the old lines than to abandon a fixed course altogether. But Burke was only one of a growing number of thinkers outside the Government circle who were becoming alive to the issues of the new age, among which the greatest was without doubt the newly conscious force of nationality. The initial efflorescence of this spirit in revolutionary France and its subsequent spread among the peoples of Europe have been described by many a writer, but the growth of the theory of nationalism in England is somewhat less familiar. As we have seen, Burke alone of the elder statesmen had shown a true apprehension of the realities of nationalism. Younger minds, held back by the Revolution and even by the Romantic movement itself, turned first towards the "philosophic" principles of liberty, equality, and fraternity. It was only when the ideas of the Revolution failed them that some at least took refuge in nationalism. Thus, whereas Burke approached the theory of nationality as a result of his meditation on political realities and in direct opposition to revolutionary ideas, his successors in England first met it as disciples of the Revolution.

The ideas of the revolutionaries were the ideas of the *philosophes* with a difference; they were the ideas of the *philosophes* deprived of their qualifying clauses, placed in an emotional instead of an intellectual setting, and transmuted by a one-sided reading of Rousseau into something that would have deeply horrified Voltaire and that did actually alienate the few men of philosophic tradition living in 1789. The world of ideas had suffered a profound change in the thirty years that followed the Seven Years War, and the author who was more than any other responsible for the change, or in whose works, at any rate, it was most clearly expressed, was Rousseau. Now Rousseau presents a difficult problem to the historian, not only because of his extraordinary eclecticism and the resulting frequent inconsistency of his opinions, but also because, as is indeed not unusual, the practical consequences of his doctrines and the popular interpretation of them were by no means what he would have wished himself. People have tried to make a revolutionary, he plaintively complained, of *"l'homme du monde qui port un plus vrai respect aux lois et aux constitutions nationales, et qui a le plus d'aversion pour les révolutions"*. Fortunately we are not concerned here with what Rousseau really believed, but with what people thought he believed. Granted that the popular view of Rousseau was a misconception, it was at all events one which had most important consequences for the history of Europe.

If people in general reduced Rousseau's opinions to a few superficial catch-words, he himself cannot altogether escape blame; for his usual literary method is to set up in a bold phrase some sweeping generalization and only subsequently to develop and qualify the idea as necessary. His readers, of course, remembered the striking phrase and forgot the qualification. "*L'homme est né libre, et partout il est dans les fers.*" After that opening, what does it matter if the rest of the book is devoted to riveting governmental chains more firmly on the people? Rousseau might have finished the *Contrat Social* with the first sentence for all effect the remainder of the book had on the minds of most of his contemporaries. Robespierre, it is true, had read rather more. Politically, too, Rousseau is not an original thinker. His influence simply lay in readjusting the emphasis on the ideas of the *philosophes* and in drawing conclusions that they had abstained from drawing. Certainly his central idea of the natural equality of man is to be found in the *philosophes*, but the tendencies of his mind combined to carry it to the border of fanaticism. The theory of the state of nature, the psychology of Locke, the Voltairean conception of humanity and reminiscences of the Sermon on the Mount, together with his own morbid vanity and self-consciousness—all went to add to the importance for him of the idea of equality. Equality was the emotional demand of his diseased nature; it was the practical demand of the unprivileged classes in France. The *ancien régime* was overthrown in the name of *Liberté, Égalité, Fraternité*, but it is the middle term that enshrined the inspiring idea of the Revolution, and in the emphasis he gave it Rousseau was acting unconsciously as the mouthpiece of the French revolutionary *bourgeoisie*. Given equality, the revolutionaries had no desire to limit the power of government; rather did they, as Burke saw, reduce all citizens to a mass of politically undifferentiated individuals in order to concentrate authority in its hands, splitting the community artificially into the individual wills and then fusing them in an authoritarian General Will. The individualist democracy of Locke passed with the *philosophes* into equalitarianism, and under the influence of Rousseau the latter was for a time confused with democracy, particularly in the minds of foreign observers. But the despotic principle of the French State soon reasserted itself, and the dictatorship of the people came to mean first the rule of a small oligarchy and then the tyranny of an emperor.

Outside France, however, the political evolution that the Republic was undergoing remained for years unrevealed, at any rate to enthusiasts for the Revolution, who took all the fine phrases of the revolutionary orators at their face value, and finally were capable of seeing in Napoleon the liberator of mankind. In England the principles of the revolutionists, as laid down especially by Rousseau, found expression in the writings of William Godwin, in particular in the famous *Political Justice*, which Pitt had refused to suppress because it was too expensive and too dull to produce any harm. As far as intrinsic value goes, it is the work of an uncritical dogmatist, but unfortunately, though Pitt was correct in refusing to attribute to it any political importance, it was by way of Godwin and his *Political Justice* that certain young men in the 'nineties came to the philosophy of the eighteenth century; and while the ideas of Godwin are uninteresting, the ideas of Coleridge, Wordsworth, and Southey are very interesting to us, as they form the sequel to the political thinking of Burke. In the beginning these

136

young poets had lapped up the pure milk of Godwinism quite uncritically, and the result had been Pantisocracy— that ideal in which the romantic enthusiasm of youth was bent to the service of an arid rationalism. Of no value in itself, Pantisocracy is the intellectual starting-place of the most significant English thinkers of the first generation of the Romantic movement. The question which inevitably presents itself, as it did when were we considering Burke, is how the mental evolution implied in that statement was possible, how the gap was bridged, how—once again—Romantic political theory was born out of the eighteenth century.

One cannot help suspecting that from the beginning the Godwinism of those who were to be the Lake Poets was different from Godwin's own; that while the phrases of Rousseau were adopted by both, they meant very different things to the French revolutionaries and to the Lake Poets. This is not to deny that our poets did not go a long way on the same road with the revolutionaries and Godwin, and of them all perhaps Wordsworth farthest. The story of his adventures in revolutionary France, his association with the Girondins of Blois and the affair of Annette, so carefully buried by his episcopal biographer, is now a more than twice-told tale, over which we need not linger long. But if we are to believe the *Prelude* the seeds of romanticism already lay germinating in his soul. Wordsworth it is in whom most clearly appears the transition from the eighteenth-century or revolutionary to the Romantic school of politics, both because we have the development of his mind traced for us by his own pen in the *Prelude* and because his *Convention of Cintra* forms the most systematic statement of what was to be the first-fruits in political thinking of the new outlook—the theory of nationality.

The great advantage which the young romanticists had in going over from the eighteenth century to the new ideas was that the terms were so often the same, though the content might be entirely contradictory. The key-word of the eighteenth century, as we have seen, is Nature, and is not Nature also the presiding deity of the Romantic movement? What matters is that the Nature of the former is a dead, rigid mechanism, while the Nature of romanticism is vital, with an organic life poured through all its parts. When Wordsworth talks of Nature he is thinking, not of algebraic formulae or geometrical propositions, not even of ethical laws and economic principles, but of the race of sun and shadow over the hills, the gentle murmur of bees or the singing of birds, all the innumerable changes of colour and sound and every transient phase of the sensual world. One may suspect that the youthful enthusiasm for Nature he acknowledges in the *Prelude* was possibly rather more highly coloured in retrospect and that it had been rather less conscious at the time. But the growing boy might easily have learnt to love the lakes and dales and wild fells of Westmorland; so well indeed that love of nature might keep the love of his fellows from expanding and allow him to grow up "remote from social life". Always with the disposition of a solitary, in the end, however, he was led by love of Nature to take an interest in man. When he gazed on the silent world of Nature, from the uttermost star to the flower at his feet, he could not but discover how

> In the midst stood Man,
> Outwardly, inwardly contemplated,
> As, of all visible natures, crown, though born
> Of dust, and kindred to the worm.(1)

It was at this stage in his mental history that Wordsworth came under the influence of Godwin and the French Revolution. He was already prepared for them, for looking through the shows of momentary phenomena he had come in a mystical and poetic fashion to a conception of the individual and humanity which appeared at first sight to be not so very different from the theory of the *philosophes*. That there was a vital difference, that the two views of humanity and nature were fundamentally alien, was only to be revealed to Wordsworth as a result of practical experience. Not only by his meditation on Nature, but also by his social environment, had he been prepared for the doctrines of the revolutionaries. Born and bred amid the rural democracy of the English Lakes, "a perfect republic of shepherds and agriculturists", departing thence for the "academic republic" of Cambridge, finally spending a considerable period in revolutionary France, he had been given as democratic an upbringing as was possible in his day.

> It could not be
> But that one tutored thus should look with awe
> Upon the faculties of man, receive
> Gladly the highest promises, and hail,
> As best, the government of equal rights
> And individual worth.(2)

Thus prepared, to the young poet, as to so many other generous minds, the Revolution came as a trumpet-call to battle, which he answered by forsaking the placid contemplation of Nature for the dust and noise of political strife. Hitherto indifferent to the prosaic studies of history and politics, now revolutionary zeal stimulated what was to be a permanent interest in these matters.

Would one have expected the boy who is portrayed in the *Prelude* to be able to say many years later that for one hour spent in the composition of poetry he had devoted twelve to the study of politics?(3) Nor was this merely an arm-chair enthusiasm. Chance alone prevented him from going to Paris with the Girondins and saved for the world a great poet in place of what one cannot but suspect would have proved a very unsuccessful and short-lived politician.

For a time Wordsworth's revolutionary enthusiasm was sufficiently violent to lead him into ways of thinking which caused him much mental anguish at the time and which he was bitterly to repent in after life; for while his French sympathies were still at their height, Pitt's Government accepted war, willingly it seemed, and joined the coalition against the new republic. In the ensuing conflict of loyalties, driven to choose between his country and liberty, the higher claim seemed the more abstract one, though Wordsworth and his friends never forgave Pitt for leading the country into courses which necessitated such a choice.

> Oh! much have they to account for, who could tear,
> By violence, at one decisive rent,
> From the best youth in England their dear pride,
> Their joy, in England; this, too, at a time
> In which worst losses easily might wear
> The best of names, when patriotic love
> Did of itself in modesty give way,
> Like the Precursor when the Deity
> Is come Whose harbinger he was; a time
> In which apostasy from ancient faith
> Seemed but conversion to a higher creed.(4)

Contemporaries could hardly be expected to know that the worst fault of the Government lay, not in its bellicose

ardour, but in obscuring its pacific intentions and a
good cause, as national causes go, by incompetent policy.
An amazing volume of invective against Pitt could be
collected from the works and letters of the Lake Poets.
For the time being they solved their political problem by
ruthlessly abandoning all patriotic sentiments and striving
to think of themselves only as citizens of the world; and
so long as the cause of liberty might be supposed to be
identified with the progress of the revolutionary armies,
this position, while uncomfortable, was fairly tenable.

The tragedy came when France in its turn alienated
their sympathies. While the glamour of republicanism
lasted English democrats remained oblivious to the
heinous offences against political morality which the
French armies were continually committing and to the
growing imperialism of the heads of the French Government. Sooner or later they were bound to be disillusioned,
and as it happened the critical event proved to be the
invasion of Switzerland and the subversion of its republican institutions by French armies in the autumn of 1798.
Then for the first time Mme de Staël wished that France
might be defeated and Carnot ventured into print in his
indignation. Only then, says Wordsworth, in his tract on
the *Convention of Cintra*, did the war begin "to be regarded
by the body of the people as indeed both just and necessary". He was thinking rather of his own frame of mind,
because the war cannot be said to have become popular
in England until after its renewal in 1803. Actually, of
course, the invasion of Switzerland was by no means the
worst crime of the young republic; but the internal
conditions of Switzerland were unknown to the outside
world, and whereas other invasions might be represented
as defensive measures undertaken against the league of

despots for the sake of freeing enslaved populations, the invasion of Switzerland was a patent interference with the internal affairs of a sister republic and the traditional home of liberty. Many English democrats managed in spite of this to retain their French sympathies; Wordsworth, along with Southey and Coleridge, was too clearsighted to continue deceiving himself. He admitted the melancholy fact:

> But now, become oppressors in their turn,
> Frenchmen had changed a war of self-defence
> For one of conquest, losing sight of all
> Which they had struggled for.(5)

To Wordsworth it was as though the foundations of the moral world had been uprooted, and he had to pass through a bitter period of disillusionment before he found anything to take the place of his revolutionary sentiments.

The process of reconciliation with his own country was assisted by his German tour in the winter of 1798; from this journey in foreign lands seems to date his realization that he still had a motherland and that the hold of England over his affections was stronger than he had known. In a well-known verse of one of the Lucy poems is reflected the awakening in his heart of patriotic sentiment, which was destined in time to fill and more than fill the void left by the collapse of republican enthusiasm. By now, moreover, the British Government, even the irrepressible Dundas, were as heartily sick of the war as was the people. Pitt resigned, peace was concluded at Amiens: England accepted the fact of the Revolution and asked only to live in concord with the new France. The Peace of Amiens, said Southey, "restored in me the English feelings which had long been deadened, and placed me in sympathy with my country". After the re-commencement of the war and the open avowal of Napoleonic imperialism, any relics of sympathy left for France vanished; there were now no stauncher patriots than Wordsworth and his friends. But something more was required before patriotism could be transformed into a definite theory of nationality, or before the lesson that Burke had vainly preached could be learned.

The imposition of a French king on Spain, resulting in the spontaneous uprising of the Spanish people in 1808, supplied that something more. The Spanish revolt aroused wild enthusiasm in England. "Even now", wrote Southey in 1816, "it is delightful to look back upon that exhilarating time, when after so long and unmitigated a season hope came upon us like the first breath of summer." The nation expanded at the promise of better things. Canning, always more alive than his colleagues to vital issues, met the new situation with the famous declaration that any nation resisting Napoleon became instantly "our essential ally".(6) With unusual rapidity an army was gathered and sent to Spain. Sir John Moore's raid on Napoleon's communications, his retreat and heroic death, followed by Wellesley's victory, roused emotion to fever pitch; then, hard on the heels of Vimiera, came the news of the Convention of Cintra. Public indig-nation knew no bounds. "No public event ever distressed me so greatly", wrote Southey.(7) Wordsworth, equally indignant, was moved to compose a tract with the object of proving that the only real hope of overthrowing Napoleon lay in the encouragement of popular risings against the French, that the movement in the Iberian peninsula was such a rising, and that the attitude adopted by the British military officers on the scene of war, as typified in the Convention of Cintra, would, if continued, be fatal to co-operation with the Spanish and Portuguese. The Convention, both Southey and Wordsworth felt, had degraded a heroic national struggle into a petty mercenary war of professional soldiers.(8) It was not that; it was something far more important, they felt. It was the appearance of a new spirit in the war against France, and what spirit but that which Burke had summoned in vain?—the spirit of a nation fighting for independence.

An incidental observation in Wordsworth's *Convention of Cintra*—"With great profit might the chiefs of the Spanish Nation look back upon the earlier part of the French Revolution"(9)—shows that, like Burke, he had grasped the secret of France's success, and the affinity between the inspiration of the revolutionary armies and the spirit of nationalism. Perhaps it was this which enabled him to pass, as he did in the course of a few years, from extreme Francophilism to equally extreme anti-Gallican nationalism. In the war in Spain it is this turning against France of her own weapon which appears most significant to Wordsworth. It reveals the inherent self-contradiction of foreign tyranny, that it is doomed to rouse the very spirit by which it must be overthrown.

> Power to the Oppressors of the world is given,
> A might of which they dream not. Oh! the curse,
> To be the awakener of divinest thoughts,
> Father and founder of exalted deeds;
> And, to whole nations bound in servile straits
> The liberal donor of capacities
> More than heroic! this to be, nor yet
> Have sense of one connatural wish, nor yet
> Deserve the least return of human thanks;
> Winning no recompense but deadly hate
> With pity mixed, astonishment with scorn!(10)

Wordsworth dates the change in the fortunes of war from the Spanish and Portuguese risings, and defends native guerrilla methods against the deprecatory opinions of British generals. But it was not the mere fighting power of Spain that mattered most. What mattered was that now Napoleon would have to face something hardly to be subdued even by the extreme of physical force, and which at last gave promise of overthrowing his Empire.

> The power of Armies is a visible thing,
> Formal, and circumscribed in time and space;
> But who the limits of that power shall trace
> Which a brave People into light can bring
> Or hide, at will,—for freedom combating
> By just revenge inflamed?(11)

This, the moral and ultimately the military influence of the peoples of Europe in their respective nations, was the force on which he based his hopes for the emancipation of Europe. From that moment when "a People, which has lived long, feels that it has a country to love, and where the heart of that People is sound", said Wordsworth, foreign dominion is destined to fall.(12)

It will be seen that the process by which the idea developed in Wordsworth's mind was very different from that which led Burke to the same conclusion. Burke had come to his theory of nationality after long reflection on man in society and the nature of the State. Wordsworth and his contemporaries did not reach their theory in this way. Wordsworth experienced the fact of nationality as a process in his own mind and confirmed it by observation of the tendencies of the world around. His patriotism was so much more than mere patriotism because the alienation of his feelings from England during the early years of the Revolutionary War meant that it appeared, not in the slow normal growth of maturing political sentiment, but as a late and conscious product of his mind. Indignation at French ambition aroused in Wordsworth, as it had roused in many of his friends, a burning patriotism combined with a violent hostility to France. Continued French aggression on the Continent led neighbouring Powers to appeal to those rights of nationality which all States had ignored and trampled on in the eighteenth century. What had been, except in Burke, only a vague sentiment in favour of the independence of nations crystallized into a definite theory as a result of the Spanish uprising and found voice in Wordsworth's prose writings and in his *Poems on National Independence and Liberty*. French disasters in Spain renewed hopes of the fall of the tyrant, which the Austrian, Russian, and Prussian movements subsequently confirmed. Thus the theory of nationality developed empirically and in two stages: the assertion of the rights of nationalities was followed by the revelation of their power. The attacks by the league of despots on the French Republic and the subsequent conquests of neighbouring peoples by the French provided an opportunity for the former, while the Peninsular War pointed to the latter.

By now it should be plain why the idea of nationality, which in Burke's day had been unknown as an explicit principle governing international behaviour, was becoming general at the end of the first decade of the nineteenth century. It remains to describe in somewhat more detail the ideas of the writer who first works out a definite theory. For Wordsworth, as for Burke, local attachment is "the tap-root of the tree of Patriotism". That was particularly true of the part of England from which Wordsworth himself came—the dales of Cumberland and Westmorland, with their tiny scattered communities of "statesmen" as they were called, small independent owner-farmers, soon, alas, to be driven out of existence as such by the increasing prosperity of the country. "Neither high-born nobleman, knight, nor esquire, was here; but many of these humble sons of the hills had a consciousness that the land, which they walked over and tilled, had for more than five hundred years been possessed by men of their name and blood."(13) This is the environment out of which Wordsworth's political theory springs; and along with local patriotism it taught him the meaning of tradition in a nation's life. He draws his conclusions in phrases that wonderfully, and surely not accidentally, echo Burke. "There is a spiritual community binding together the living and the dead, the good, the brave, and the wise, of all ages."(14) To Wordsworth, as to Burke, tradition is essential to a nation. How well he knew "the solemn fraternity which a great Nation composes— gathered together, in a stormy season, under the shade of ancestral feeling".(15) He cries, as the shadow of Napoleon looms over his mind, "Perdition to the Tyrant who would wantonly cut off an independent nation from its inheritance in past ages".(16)

Again, as with Burke, this view of the nation proves incompatible with the arid individualism of the eighteenth century. "The vigour of the human soul", says Wordsworth, "is from without and from futurity,—in breaking down limit, and losing and forgetting herself in the sensation and image of Country and of the human race."(17) The influence of his religious beliefs, Coleridge's new idealistic philosophy, of which more anon, the political teaching of Burke, and practical experience—all combined to force on Wordsworth the conviction that a man cannot live to himself, that his individuality is never more fully expressed than when he takes unto himself national and traditional feeling, until ultimately each separate soul is an epitome of humanity. This is not a denial of individuality, but its true fulfilment: far from being incompatible with the independence of the individual man or nation, it is only to be realized in a condition of such independence. And where the nation is not free the individual members of it are not free, since national independence is "the underground root of the tree of liberty", which without it cannot flourish. "For little has that man understood the majesty of true national freedom, who believes that a population, like that of Spain, in a country like that of Spain, may want the qualities needful to fight out their independence, and yet possess the excellencies which render men susceptible of true liberty."(18)

The moral necessity of national independence being thus established, its application to international relations follows automatically. Every community which claims the right of nationality for itself necessarily should recognize the same rights in other communities. "The man, who in this age feels no regret for the ruined honour of other Nations, must be poor in sympathy for the honour of his own Country."(19) Moreover, it is to the interest of every independent nation to maintain the independence of other nations; this is particularly true of Great Britain, which can only thus be safeguarded from the danger of a continental empire. The implications of this view we see when in the *Convention of Cintra* Wordsworth comes to discuss the problem of the remaking of Europe that would confront the Allied statesmen after Napoleon had been defeated; he proposes a solution that anticipates in all essentials the doctrine later to be associated with the name of Mazzini. "The materials of a new balance of power", he writes, "exist in the language, and name, and territory of Spain, in those of France and those of Italy, Germany, Russia, and the British Isles. The smaller States must disappear, and merge in the large nations and widespread languages. The possibility of this remodelling of Europe I see clearly; earnestly do I pray for it."(20) A significant omission is the Austrian Empire. Again, "It will be a happy day for Europe, when the natives of Italy and the natives of Germany (whose duty is, in like manner, indicated to them) shall each dissolve the pernicious barriers which divide them and form themselves into a mighty People."(21) "I wish to see Spain, Italy, France, Germany, formed into independent nations; nor have I any desire to reduce the power of France further than may be necessary for that end."(22)

Wordsworth did not abandon his ideals at the end of the war; for believing as he did that its victorious issue was to be attributed to the strength of popular sentiment, and not to the efforts of kings and emperors, on this account he called for generous recognition of the rights of nations by rulers whom their subjects had saved from destruction. Wordsworth, unlike Burke, was not entirely alone; there were a few others in 1815 who dreamed with him of rebuilding Europe on a new principle of nationality and not on the principles of the Holy Alliance. Southey, in a letter to Scott, expresses similar ideas. He suggests that France should be reduced to the boundaries of 1660, that North Germany should be unified under Prussia, Italy consolidated into one kingdom, and Poland re-established.(23) Among Tory politicians Canning was perhaps unique in recognizing that the war had been "a war of the people",(24) that the spirit of national independence alone had been powerful enough to overthrow Napoleon, and that nations had not only been saved but created in the struggle. "Germany", he said in 1813, "is now a nation as well as a name."(25)

But in the Tory reaction after the Peace liberal sentiments became obscured, and even Wordsworth and his friends began to look with favour on the Holy Alliance and to approve of foreign intervention against struggling nationalities. Canning was in this respect more faithful to the promises of the war, but so only blackened his record in the eyes of men who earlier had shared with him the vision of the meaning of nationality. To the disappointment of many Wordsworth turned more and more away from idealistic politics, until the erstwhile revolutionary was to be found exerting his public influence in defence of such institutions as capital punishment, slavery, and the legal immunity of cruelty to animals. His great friend, Henry Crabb Robinson, wrote in 1826 to Dorothy Wordsworth: "I assure you it gives me real pain when I think that some future commentator may possibly hereafter write—'This great poet survived to the fifth decennary of the nineteenth Century, but he appears to have dyed in the year 1814 as far as life consisted in an active sympathy with the temporary welfare of his fellow creatures—He had written heroically and divinely against the tyranny of Napoleon, but was quite indifferent to all the successive tyrannies which disgraced the succeeding times—The Spaniards the moment they were under the yoke of the most odious and contemptible tyrant that ever breathed—ceased to be objects of interest—The Germans who emancipated themselves were most

ungratefully neglected by their sovereigns and the poet—
The Greeks began a War as holy as that of the Spaniards
He was silent—He had early manifested a feeling for the
negroes and the poet did honour to his friend Clarkson—
That source of sympathetic tears was dried up—A new
field of enterprise was opened in America—The poet's
eye was not a prophetic one.' . . ." (26) The sequel is
told in a letter of Wordsworth's: "My sister had taken
flight for Herefordshire when *your* letter, for such we
guessed it to be, arrived—it was broken open (pray
forgive the offence) and all your charges of concealment
and reserve frustrated. . . . Your supposed Biography
entertained me much. I could give you the other side.—
farewell. W. W."(27)

Doubtless a defence could be put up for Wordsworth,
but whatever the other side might be it was plain that his
political idealism had died by the end of the struggle
with Napoleon. As for Blois and the Girondin club, they
had receded almost as far into the distance as poor Annette:
the ageing poet could only marvel how it had come to
pass that *he* should have behaved thus—when all the
world was young. Even nationalism, second efflorescence
of his poetic soul, by degrees lost its glamour. Before
middle age had descended on him he was an old man at
heart, dead the fire that had flamed so brightly. In the
Convention of Cintra, the high-water mark of his significance as a political citizen, and in the *Sonnets on National
Independence and Liberty*, was enshrined most gloriously
the passing moment of the nation's history. "Wordsworth
alone", declares Swinburne, "could put into his verse
the whole soul of a nation armed or arming for self-devoted
self-defence; could fill his meditation with the spirit of
a whole people, that in the act of giving it a voice and an

expression he might inform and renovate that spirit with the purity and sublimity of his own."(28) That phase ended, the nation went on—without Wordsworth.

NOTES

I   1. Prelude VIII. 485–8.
     2. Id. IX. 238–43.
     3. In 1833. Quoted, Harper: Wordsworth, II. 385 (1916).
     4. Prelude X. 300–310.
     5. Id. XI. 206–9.
     6. Canning: Speeches, 1828, II. 352 (June 15, 1808).
     7. D. Stuart: Letters from the Lake Poets (1889), 397. Jan. 13, 1809.
     8. Southey: Life and Corr. (1849), III. 176.
     9. Wordsworth: Prose Works (ed. Knight, 1896), Convention of Cintra, I. 262.
    10. Excursion VII. 821–31.
    11. Poems dedicated to National Independence and Liberty, Part II, No. 32 (1811).
    12. Conventions of Cintra; 247. cf. D. Stuart, op. cit. 418; Southey: Life and Corr. III. 155; Letter to Capt. Pasley, 314 (in Wordsworth's Prose Works).
    13. Prose Works, II. 63.
    14. Convention of Cintra, 272.
    15. Id. 227.
    16. Id. 257.
    17. Id. 208.
    18. Id. 131.
    19. Id. 258.
    20. Prose Works, I. 317.
    21. Convention of Cintra, 252.
    22. Letter to Capt. Pasley, Prose Works. I. 315.
    23. Southey: Life and Corr. IV. 96 (Dec. 1814).
    24. Canning: Speeches in Liverpool (1825), 94 (Jan. 10, 1814).

25. Canning: Speeches (1828), III. 436 (Nov. 17, 1813).
26. Correspondence of Henry Crabb Robinson with the Wordsworth Circle (ed. E. J. Morley, 1927), I. 153-4.
27. Id. 159-61.
28. Swinburne: Miscellanies, 149-50 (1886).

CHAPTER VI

THE POLITICAL PHILOSOPHY OF COLERIDGE

WORDSWORTH'S, WE HAVE SAID, was a light
that failed. After the great years he went on turning out
verse and occasionally fulminating on political events
from his Lake fortress; unconscious that, as the generous
ardours of youth had faded, inspiration had fled and
returned to him but rarely. The nation, too, was settling
down to a more sober mood. War was becoming a hum-
drum affair, losing both its horror and glamour. It was
obvious that Napoleon must be resisted, yet who could
remain enthusiastic in support of such Governments as
England knew? Even ultimate triumph could cast few
laurels on their fated brows. The soul of the nation, sound
in the darkest days of the war, began to waver when
victory had been won and miseries endured for the sake
of victory were perpetuated and intensified in peace.
Many must have thought in the years after Waterloo that
the soul of England had been stifled for ever by war and
repression. The inspiration of the Whigs seemed to have
died with Charles James Fox, while the Tory party's
promise for the future was still in the wilderness with
Canning. The vitality of the nation spent itself in the
undisciplined heavings of the masses, finding articulate
utterance only through the gargantuan thunderings of
Cobbett; against which volcanic simmerings the governing
classes could find no defence but to draw closer war
controls, to shut off the vents, repress and repress.

Meanwhile, what of those who like Wordsworth had
started out so bravely to remake the world in the early
'nineties? The French Revolution had passed away from

their sympathies long ago; blissful dawn had grown to a dire and tempestuous day; while liberal Europe still lurked in conventicles and taverns, not yet graduated from the status of conspiracy. For men who were constrained to think, who could not, like the remnant of the Whigs, save their independence by erecting party into a principle, there seemed no choice but to rally under the banner of the utilitarians and economists. The prospect may not seem one calculated to inspire generous minds. The youth of the country, nevertheless, turned towards the philosophic radicals in preference to joining the leaderless and policyless Whigs, and Tories whose highness and dryness had been accentuated almost beyond the bounds of credibility by the war. Periods of stress always heighten political distinctions in the long run, even when the immediate danger is sufficiently great to force a temporary and superficial coalition. The peculiarity of the situation that developed after the war was that, although in their specific doctrines the Whigs were nearer to the Tories than they were to the Radicals, so great was the power of the traditional party cleavage that they accepted the alliance of the Radicals and took up, after long hesitation, certain radical measures, rather than lose their party identity by becoming absorbed in the Tories.

For a generation the political history of the country is almost monopolized by the struggle over Reform and Repeal, which once more divided Parliament into sharply defined parties. Historians have accepted for general purposes a division which simplifies their work so considerably. In consequence utilitarianism, the only theoretic movement of the period which even in appearance fits in with the political division, has received its due meed of attention; but until recently the other forces which took part in shaping the national development have been neglected. To-day we have learnt to appreciate the greater complexity of history and to look deeper than the mimic warfare of party politics. Professor Wallas has laid bare some of the secret springs of political action in his biography of Francis Place; the Webbs have narrated the early struggles of trade unionism; and justice has tardily been done to Robert Owen and William Cobbett in several biographies. Professor Webster and Dr. Temperley have thrown light on the principles behind British foreign policy, while Professor Halévy, with the advantage of an external standpoint, has shown us how largely the Methodist influence figures in determining the trend of opinion. It is worth remarking that all these lie outside party categories, and also that rightly understood they are all essentially practical—economic and ethical—rather than theoretic developments.

Had thinking on politics, we are compelled to ask, ceased outside utilitarian circles? One did not expect it from othodox Whigs and Tories, but had Burke's genius been entirely wasted? Everyone knows, of course, his influence on the party system, on colonial policy, and so forth. Then again, the previous chapter would not be where it is if we did not think that in the *Convention of Cintra* Wordsworth was carrying on and developing a theory, or perhaps an attitude of mind, that might be found in the great political philosopher of his youth. But was this all? Is there no school to which we can point as continuing the tradition established by Burke? English thinking has not in general favoured the development of schools, and the search is vain. If there was no school, however, there were two individuals at least whom we can mark out as descendants of Burke, the one in practical politics, the other in theory—George Canning and Samuel Taylor Coleridge; and with Coleridge we may at any rate group Wordsworth and Southey. With Canning's political ideals and his obligations to Burke we have no space here to deal; moreover, as befitted one of the greatest of British Foreign Ministers, he has by now received as adequate an interpretation as history is likely to provide. Coleridge offers a more untilled field, and to him we turn, knowing that for the history of thought a single individual may well be far more important than whole shoals of 'ians and 'ites. We shall see that the idea of the nation, found already in Burke and Wordsworth, is further elaborated by Coleridge, and takes a definite step forward. What had been in Burke a prophetic inspiration and in Wordsworth a practical deduction from certain facts of experience, took on a fuller and more philosophic meaning in Coleridge, and was put forward more consciously as an alternative to prevailing political theories.

I

PHILOSOPHY AND POLITICS

Coleridge's political evolution runs parallel to that of Wordsworth and Southey. Along with them, after a period of revolutionary zeal, he had recanted, or as he put it himself, "I have snapped my squeaking baby-trumpet of sedition, and the fragments lie scattered in the lumber-room of penitence".(1) Like Wordsworth, he had been in consequence "wearied with politics, even to soreness". Again like Wordsworth, the Napoleonic War roused his latent patriotism and induced him to lend the aid of his pen to the Government in its struggle against the Emperor. For a period he became a most energetic journalist and pamphleteer, and not an ineffective one: Daniel Stuart said he would sooner have Coleridge as his leader-writer than any other living writer. However, the poet-philosopher's literary support was not adequately appreciated by the Tory Government, which left him at the end of the war, he complained, unrewarded and undefended from the malice of the enemies he had made in the service of Church and State. Perhaps his own dubious political allegiance had something to do with that. He never really lived down Pantisocracy, and it had hardly been high political support to write of a Government:

> It vexed his soul to see
> So grand a Cause, so proud a realm,
> With Goose or Goody at the helm;
> Who long ago had fall'n asunder
> But for their rival's baser blunder,
> The coward whine and Frenchified
> Slaver and slang of the other side.(2)

The fact is that Coleridge, as he himself many times claimed, was at no stage in his career a real party man. But we need not on this account go so far as Halévy, who calls him "*un excentrique, un isolé. Il ne se rattache à nul corps constitué, à nulle tradition nationale.*"(3) If he found himself ploughing a lonely furrow it was because he was pioneering in new ground while his fellows were following the old ruts, not because of mere innate perversity of temperament. He was eclectic, it is true, but that was by force of circumstance. Coleridge, said Poole, "endeavouring to discover *Truth*, found her in Fragments scattered among all".(4) That is indeed in itself sufficient to account for his failure in politics; it is not discreet to place devotion to truth above party loyalty or to approach politics with the attitude of a philosopher—unless one is a philosopher king. Politicians as a race, in spite of a few notable exceptions, have never taken kindly to philosophizing. Burke—who could assume almost too successfully the pose of Philistinism—had found himself a Triton of the mind amid intellectual minnows, and if even he suffered misunderstanding and despiteous treatment, what could but be the fate of Coleridge, who never compromised for the sake of appearances, never sacrificed philosophy at the altar of common sense? Indeed, we must confess that he delighted rather overmuch to shroud himself in the mantle of metaphysical obscurity. Not that Coleridge was altogether to blame for the lack of appreciation with which his attempt to introduce an idealistic philosophy was greeted, for it was not until the end of the nineteenth century that it gradually dawned upon English thinkers that in ignoring Idealism they were living in a lost world, philosophically speaking.

Of course, to begin with Coleridge had adopted Godwinism, than which nothing could be farther from the spirit of idealist philosophy. But even while his intellect was still held in bonds by the system of Hartley and Godwin, Coleridge had confessed to a love for "Plato's gorgeous nonsense". After a period of eclipse practically coterminous with the dominance of the school of Locke, as philosophy was beginning to recover from the blight of common sense, the Platonic spirit was reviving. The powerful mind of Kant had worked out a system which, by basing knowledge firmly on the *a priori* synthesis, had reintroduced idealism, and his writings were steadily making their way among German thinkers, though Coleridge seems to have drawn his inspiration rather from the lesser disciples of Kant, such as Schelling, than from the fountain-head. However, when in revulsion from politics he turned to the study of the new German metaphysics, he was almost the first thinker of importance in the British Isles to become aware of their significance. His mind had been prepared by research in such unfrequented fields as were then the writings of the Neoplatonists, the mediaeval schoolmen and Spinosa. One part of his life-work was the endeavour to build up on the most miscellaneous foundations a new transcendental philosophy, with which he hoped to reconcile a reinterpreted and purified Pauline Christianity.

But his very receptivity to new ideas was a fatal barrier to the development of a clear-cut philosophical system, for Idealism was not the only new movement that was stirring in Europe at the beginning of the nineteenth century. Contemporaneously the religious revival was gathering force, while Scriptural criticism, on the other hand, was also entering on a new phase, science was at the opening of an era of unprecedented progress, evolution was in the air, the flame of nationalism was burning brightly, European literature had been swept by Romanticism: and in all these movements Coleridge was a sharer. The new developments in philosophy, religion, and science all demanded his allegiance, and to the union of these three so often antagonistic studies in a single system he devoted indefatigable labour. The effort was foredoomed to failure, but it may help us to appreciate the difficulties of the task if we reflect that the work of the whole subsequent century has only served to intensify the difficulties and make the ultimate reconciliation seem farther off than ever.

Coleridge's starting-points were the soul and God—the individual consciousness and the Absolute, as a philosopher might call them. Scientific psychology was to reveal the former, idealist philosophy, together with religious inspiration, the latter, and the whole was to be unified under the aegis of a mystical Christianity. This ambitious scheme was, alas, except for a few scattered fragments, never to be realized; but throughout his life Coleridge cherished the dream of success, and in the meantime directed his great conversational and literary powers to the instruction of his fellow-countrymen in the mysteries of the new metaphysic. In vain: there is no evidence that a single person understood him, and the day of Idealism had to be postponed until Bradley and his disciples arrived to rescue English thought from the dead hand of Utilitarianism. Coleridge was altogether out of place in the England of the Prince Regent—a fact which we cannot regard as entirely to his discredit. In many of his opinions he had followers, isolated or in small groups, but in philosophy he found few to sympathize with him, none to understand; and this despite the little company of half-bewildered listeners who gathered round him at Highgate and endured those eternal discourses about "om-m-mjects" and "sum-m-mjects" so cruelly satirized by that fountain of philosophic wisdom, Thomas Carlyle.

The divorce of philosophy and religion from politics was in Coleridge's view one of the cardinal faults of the age. For, he claims, all epoch-making revolutions are coincident with, and undoubtedly consequent on, the rise

and fall of metaphysical systems.(5) This may be stated
in an extreme manner, but in so far as its meaning is
that the theories of an age about itself and about the ends
of its existence are a most important factor in the practical
working out of its destiny, it is patently true. Whether
they will or no, men cannot live from hand to mouth
intellectually: if they do not evolve a good philosophy
they will fall victims to a bad one. But a philosophy of
some sort they must and will have, because the problems
with which the *Zeitgeist* is concerned are essentially
problems of philosophy. Not that the mass of mankind
will ever devote a moment's thought to speculative
philosophy: the ideas that dictate the course of the world's
history have their essential being at each particular stage
in the minds of those individuals who are world leaders
in thought and action. Even great men may be barely
conscious of the purposes they are serving, the principles
they obey. But Coleridge holds that without an habitual
interest in the ultimate. problems of philosophy and
ethics no man can be a great statesman, and that even
for the attainment of mére material prosperity pure speculation is essential.(6) It was hardly likely that he should
find much recognition of these views in Georgian England.
"At present the more effective a man's talents are, and
the more likely he is to be useful and distinguished in the
highest situations of public life, the earlier does he show
his aversion to the metaphysics and the books of metaphysical speculation which are placed before him. . . .
The living of former ages communed gladly with a
life-breathing philosophy. The living of the present
age wisely leave the dead to take care of the dead."(7)
He compares the politicians of his own day with men such
as Lorenzo the Magnificent, Count Mirandola, Sir Philip

Sidney, and Milton, and can afford to leave the contrast to speak for itself. "We want *thinking* Souls," is his cry, "We *want them*."(8)

Despite the contempt which early nineteenth-century England had for the philosophy of Idealism its influence on political thinking is not to be denied, and it forms an important element in that revolt against eighteenth-century ideas which we are studying. What, indeed, could be more opposed to the individualistic world of the eighteenth century, with mind and matter each divided up into sharp, separate, impenetrable entities, than the eternal ebb and flow of the philosophy of the Absolute? And it needed to be mentioned here because, although Coleridge is not to be reckoned in the full sense of the word an Idealist philosopher, his studies in the new German metaphysics undoubtedly left their mark on his political thinking.

II

NATURAL RIGHTS AND EXPEDIENCY

If what we have said above constituted all there is to be said of Coleridge as a political thinker, the reader might justly ask what he is doing in the line of succession to Burke instead of being classed among the dervishes of the pure reason. But in the first place we must note that the influence he desired to see exercised by philosophy was over the minds of men, and not over the details of politics. Philosophy dealt in ends, it did not prescribe the means to their attainment; and although his ideal statesmen would be philosopher kings, metaphysics was not on that account to form the immediate groundwork of politics.(1) For systems which pretended to evolve systems of politics out of the pure reason he had only the contemptuous designation, "metapolitics". "The moral laws of the intellectual world," he writes, "as far as they are deducible from pure intellect, are never perfectly applicable to our mixed and sensitive nature, because man is something besides reason; because his reason never acts by itself, but must clothe itself in the substance of individual understanding and specific inclination, in order to become a reality and an object of consciousness and experience."(2) In other words, the reason, when it is laying down laws and principles, is generalizing, whereas the reality of experience is to be found only in the individual and particular. Forgetfulness of this fact, or unwillingness to admit it, has led many philosophers astray when they have dealt· with politics. It forms one of the most important and certainly one of the most effective items in Croce's criticism of Hegel, and it is a testimony to the penetration of Coleridge that he should have pointed out so early the main weakness of the political theory of idealist philosophers. Primarily he is attacking Rousseau and the method of argument followed to a considerable degree in the *Contrat Social*, but, as Maitland observes, the criticism is equally applicable to the political theory of Kant, and, we may add, still more to that of Hegel. Far from revolting against Burke's view, then, we find that Coleridge supplies the argued justification for Burke's instinctive distrust of the uncorroborated logical intellect. He follows him, too, in protesting with all his force against that political theory of abstract or natural rights which is the result of "metapolitical" arguments. To use

164

Burke's own words, they are both suspicious of the application of the so-called rights of man to the positive laws of civil society. Only fiends or angels, said Coleridge, could order their lives on the principles of the abstract reason, and though he does not say so, his opinion is obviously that if mankind tries the experiment it will be towards the former rather than the latter that it will gravitate.

Burke and Coleridge had a colossal experiment on these lines before their eyes and in the end their verdicts are nearly identical, though for a few years Coleridge had seemed to be one of the rising hopes of the English Jacobins. We need not, of course, suspect him of disingenuousness when he declares in a letter of 1798 that his opinions were never tainted in any degree by the French system. Nevertheless, one cannot be doubtful on which side his sympathies had been in the early revolutionary war, or what had been his attitude towards the anti-Jacobin persecutions. In 1800 he wrote, "Jacobinism in England can scarcely be said to exist, otherwise than as an abusive epithet".(3) The errors of the anti-Jacobins seemed to him as gross as those of their opponents and far less excusable. They had betrayed a callousness to the sufferings of the French people and indifference to the crimes of the *ancien régime* which had also been the greatest defect in Burke's *Reflections*; and they had undermined English institutions by pretending that those of France had been on the same high level of excellence. The anti-Jacobins, he wrote in the *Friend*, like their opponents, worshipped a mere abstraction; they made the rights of sovereigns supreme and treated kingdoms and peoples as if they were the private property of their rulers. Their policy involved the adoption against Jacobinism of its own worst methods, and by a systematic and unjustified repression provided it with allies and excuses. Stirring it up in the first place for party reasons, the propagators of the anti-Jacobin scare had ended by sharing in it themselves, and their political judgments had in consequence been subject to amazing aberrations. Even Burke had written as though he deemed perpetual and organized anarchy a possibility in France. Finally, by underestimating the attractions of Jacobinism its opponents had played into its hands. It was unwise, Coleridge rightly said, to represent a political system as attracting only fools and knaves when experience had shown its greatest danger to be that it had a particular fascination for noble and imaginative minds.(4)

These criticisms of the anti-Jacobins, however, are gradually forgotten in a rising tide of denunciation of Jacobinism itself. The explanation of the increasing conservatism of Coleridge is that the evolution of his political opinions almost exactly reverses the general trend of public opinion in England. Whilst the Jacobin panic fostered by Pitt and Burke had been at its height, Coleridge had rightly scorned the possibility of revolution in England. During the dark years that followed the Treaty of Vienna he learned to think more highly of Burke's diagnosis: alarm at the growth of what he called Jacobinism is the root of much in Coleridge's later opinions. The impression left on the English mind by the Reign of Terror cannot easily be understood by us to-day. Coleridge, who had escaped the panic when all around were scenting treason and Jacobinism in every corner, with a contrariety which may have been perverseness or which may have been insight, began, as soon as the anti-Jacobin cry had died down, to discover some need for it, and by the time of the after-war distresses was in a very fever of apprehension, which haunted him to the end of his days. He was particularly unfortunate in that he was continually having to turn round in the midst of his outbursts against Jacobinism to defend himself from the charge of having once belonged himself to the subversive brotherhood. His case is that Jacobinism, weakest during the days of panic in the 'nineties, has not perished, but has sunk from the men of letters to the labouring classes, and in becoming less conspicuous has become more dangerous.(5) In particular, he singles out the new societies of mechanics—trade unions, we should call them—as Jacobinical: by their very existence, he says, they dislocate the ordered and beneficent interdependence of classes,(6) a remark revealing the attitude of mind which could lead the most benevolent of men to oppose bitterly combinations of workers. The effects of Jacobinism, to continue with Coleridge's thesis, are to be traced in the social disorder and dissoluteness of the lower classes, but not in them alone. It is also manifested in the dissenting movement, in the dis-rustication of the country gentry, and in the tendency of one political party to merge everything in personal rights.(7)

Coleridge claims to have been the first to analyse the phenomena of Jacobinism, distinguishing the Jacobin from the republican and the democrat, as well as from the mere demagogue,(8) but his description is in essentials the same as Burke's. Like him he finds the root of Jacobinism in the despotism of the abstract reason, the erection of government by means of mob violence on so-called natural rights, instead of on social privilege, positive institutions, and experience. "For Jacobinism is *monstrum. hybridum*, made up in part of despotism and in part of

abstract reason misapplied to objects that belong entirely
to experience and the understanding. Its instincts and
mode of action are in strict correspondence with its
origin. In all places Jacobinism betrays its mixed parentage
and nature, by applying to the brute passions and physical
force of the multitude (that is, to man as a mere animal), in
order to build up government and the frame of society
on natural rights instead of social privileges, on the universals of abstract reason instead of positive institutions,
the lights of specific experience, and the modifications
of existing circumstances."(9) Jacobinism, again, always
talks of rights instead of duties, and amongst rights only
recognizes those of individuals. It believes that the
happiness and misery of the people depend on Governments, and because Governments are always selfish allows
none to be rightful unless based on universal suffrage.
Hence a Jacobinical Government is simply the populace
personified, "a multitudinous idol". The existing State
being sacrificed in the name of individual rights,
individuals are incorporated in a new State, which, as
Coleridge, like Burke, understands, is a thousand times
more oppressive.(10)

Thus Coleridge's criticism of Jacobinism resolves
itself into a criticism of democracy, connecting the anti-
Jacobinism of the 'nineties with the resistance to the
Reform Bill. On the democratic theory, says Coleridge,
there is no stopping-place short of universal suffrage,
and then he adds as a *reductio ad absurdum*, women would
have as great a claim as men to the vote. What reason,
he asks fairly enough, can the French revolutionaries
give for excluding women from the franchise? The fact
is, according to Coleridge, that there are differences of
degree between human beings, whereas the system of

individual representation rests on the principle that reason is not susceptible of degree, and that politics should be an expression of the pure reason. On this account alone democracy is bound to fail. This is the fundamental principle on which all the disciples of Burke fall foul of the revolutionaries and democrats, because it is the basis of what Coleridge calls "the mad and barbarizing scheme of a delegation of individuals". "There is no unity for a people but in a representation of national interests; a delegation from the passions or wishes of the individuals themselves is a rope of sand."(11) Direct representation is untenable in theory and impracticable in fact. A pure democracy would be nothing less than a Church, the distinction between a State and a Church being that the former is based on classes, interests, unequal property, whereas the latter is founded on the equality before God of all mankind. Equality is not a possibility in political society, which implies, in fact which essentially is, governed society; and government means aristocracy, the only alternative to which is "fool-and-knave-ocracy".(12) The improvement of human life depends on the few in all ages, and a national constitution is the work of the few who are wiser and better than their fellows.(13) At heart Coleridge is hostile to democracy for the same reason as Burke: they both disbelieved in human nature and distrusted the political capacity of the average man.

Following the Whig tradition as well as revolutionary doctrine, Coleridge taught that great respect should be paid to the opinion of the people. But, like Burke, he drew a distinction between the "people" and the whole population of the country, which though not very clear seemed to him vital at a time when every mob was arrogating to itself the "sacred name of people". The distinction, according to Coleridge, was that the people is governed by virtue and reason, whereas mobs are essentially irrational. "The passions, like a fused metal, fill up the wide interstices of thought and supply the defective links: and thus incompatible assertions are harmonized by the sensation, without the sense, of connection."(14) We can understand why the appeal to the mob seemed to him the greatest sin of the Whigs in the passing of the Reform Bill, because it involved, he feared, the introduction in England of that subordination of the legislature to physical force which had been the cause of untold evil throughout Europe. Coleridge's distinction between the people and the mob is rather abstract in form, nor do any other of the Tories assist us to a definition, in spite of their fondness for using the distinction. Burke's conception of what comprised the "people" we have already examined and perhaps found not very helpful, and it is evident that Coleridge finds even more difficulty than Burke in expressing his meaning. Possibly there is room for doubt whether he has a meaning at all. As Rousseau's General Will is an attempt to combine faith in the divine inspiration of democracy with considerable suspicion of the terrestrial wisdom of the voters at political elections, so Burke's and Coleridge's "people" is an attempt to single out that part of the nation possessing constitutional sagacity for the grant of political power. It is an attempt to reconcile a consciousness of the power of public opinion with fear of Jacobinism.

Coleridge hovered between a faith in human nature derived from both the *philosophes* and from romanticism and the traditional Tory distrust of human nature, though the latter tended to prevail as time went on. In the first

170

edition of the *Friend* he had contradicted Johnson's opinion that the mass of the people suffer from "plebeian envy"; a note of 1818 withdraws the more generous observation. To those who would rouse the populace he propounds a dilemma: if the people are really good and wise, why should they be discontented; if ignorant and miserable, how can they be appealed to as judges?(15) The latter is undoubtedly the truer alternative; if there is wickedness in the people, he knows there is much more misery—not to be remedied, though, by inflaming their passions and teaching them to rebel. The true lover of his kind pleads *for* the poor and ignorant, not *to* them. Illumination must precede revolution. "There is no slight danger from general ignorance: and the only choice, which Providence has graciously left to a vicious government, is either to fall by the people, if they are suffered to become enlightened, or with them, if they are kept enslaved and ignorant."(16) It is curious that Coleridge failed to take the one step farther and realize, as perhaps Voltaire alone had realized already, that illumination would in itself be the social revolution, that indeed it is the only kind of revolution with any possibility of true success—but this is a conception to which the world has been slow in giving allegiance. It was something that Coleridge was sufficiently a child of the eighteenth century to attach supreme importance to enlightenment, and that he retained enough of the influence of Rousseau to believe that it could and should be extended to all.

We see that Coleridge's theory is on the whole extremely undemocratic. Two criticisms occur naturally to the modern reader. First, the conception of democracy here denounced seems very different from the modern interpretation of the term. The answer is that as actually held then it was, and that if to-day we realize more clearly both the possibilities and the limitations of the political organization of the people, it is to be attributed in no small degree to the work of those thinkers, like Burke and Coleridge, who exposed the shallowness of the Utilitarian and Revolutionary conceptions of democracy. Again, it may be urged that he assumes the populace must always remain the illiterate and disorderly mob that the eighteenth century knew too well. Burke would have agreed that they must. But in the generation that followed him the Radicals and a certain section of the Tories, including Coleridge, had begun to grasp the function that education was to play in the modern world. How far Coleridge went towards the theory of education as making the world safe for democracy we shall see in the next chapter. He can hardly be blamed for foreseeing all too clearly the years that were to pass before even an approximation to an educated democracy became a possibility.

Jacobinism, then, and the political philosophy of natural rights, together with the crude conceptions of democracy for which they were responsible, are decisively rejected by Coleridge, and having disposed thus completely of abstract right, nothing remains for him but to transfer political questions to the ground of expediency. Contrary to what we should expect from a disciple of the idealist philosophy, he is willing to modify every principle according to the circumstances of its political application. He professes himself "a zealous advocate for deriving the various forms and modes of government from human prudence, and of deeming that to be just which experience has proved to be expedient".(17) Burke himself could say no more.

Are we to conclude, then, that having rejected the

politics of natural right Coleridge turned to Utilitarianism, substituting for the natural man of Rousseau the average man of Bentham? Yet he and his friends never wearied of abusing the utilitarian morality of the age— a degradation of human nature, an apotheosis of selfishness, encouraging perpetual fear and suspicion of the designs of our neighbours, and denying morality by reducing it to a calculation of consequences. To make some consequent reward or penalty the motive of moral action was a good principle for the law, but fatal to true morality; to do good, as less rigorous Utilitarians pretended, for the pleasure of having a good conscience, was to abrogate the conscience altogether.(18) For the ethical teaching of revealed religion, as well as for moral and political philosophy, he said, utilitarianism substituted a "guess-work of general consequences", which would be an inadequate guide even if one could assume that the actions resulting from prudent self-interest would always coincide with those dictated by conscience.(19) Instead of relying on the common conscience of mankind, an abstract and unstable criterion would be set up in the varying opinions of every individual; for that reason, if for no other, Coleridge argues, utilitarian morality will not work. Southey's comment is even more to the point. "He who maintains that men are best directed by a sense of their own interest, should be prepared to show that they always know what their own interests really are. The sense of duty is more influential in good men, envy, hatred, and malice, in wicked ones; prejudice in many, superstition in more, passion in most men."(20)

Coleridge agrees with the Utilitarians, as indeed Burke did, that the object of government is to secure the greatest possible happiness for the greatest possible number, but he proceeds to show that for practical purposes the Hedonist criterion of good is almost meaningless. "Don't you see", he asks, "the ridiculous absurdity of setting up *that* as a principle or motive of action, which is, in fact, a necessary and essential instinct of our very nature—an inborn and inextinguishable desire? How can creatures susceptible of pleasure and pain do otherwise than desire happiness? But *what* happiness? That is the question. . . . Your fine maxim is so very true as to be a mere truism."(21) All the utilitarian principle comes to, then, is that there *is* in human life an ultimate good, though the majority of mankind may be ignorant of its nature, a *summum bonum*, at which we should according to the best of our lights aim. This end we can, if we like, call happiness, and on one occasion Coleridge even defines happiness in terms of pleasure, as "the continuity and sum-total of the pleasure which is allotted or happens to a man". Pleasure, he continues, is "the harmony between the specific excitability of a living creature, and the exciting causes correspondent thereto".(23) Here he seems in danger of falling into the Hedonist fallacy of making happiness the sum of pleasures, thus constructing the universal by simple addition of particulars. Elsewhere he corrects himself: "Happiness in general may be defined, not the aggregate of pleasurable sensations—for this is either a dangerous error and the creed of sensualists, or else a mere translation or wordy paraphrase—but the state of that person who, in order to enjoy his nature in the highest manifestations of conscious *feeling*, has no need of doing wrong, and who, in order to do right, is under no necessity of abstaining from enjoyment."(24) It is the condition, in other words, of the idealist free will. Viewed in this light it is seen that

174

happiness can be founded on virtue alone, for it consists in the activity of the good self—"the self whose end and pleasure is the realization of the ideal self".(25) Thus the elusive intuitional criterion of good comes in again, to the total discomfiture of utilitarian ethics.

In spite of this conclusive demolition of the utilitarian theory, Coleridge's legislative criterion remains utility, or, to use Burke's term, expediency. Individual differences do not seem to him so great as to prohibit any attempt at a systematic treatment of the units comprising political society. There is no avoiding the fact that for purposes of law-making men have to be considered in the mass. And since, whatever else they are, the majority are partly selfish, and action resulting from self-interest can be calculated far more easily than any other, Coleridge concludes that this is the motive on which the statesman can most safely rely in legislating.(26)

To a certain extent, thus, Coleridge is utilitarian. We must return to his consideration of natural rights for a moment in order to point out that to a certain extent also he may be said to believe in natural rights; in fact, he combines what is most reasonable in both political views. We have shown how he attacks the rights of nature school; but although he did not clearly recognize the distinction himself, Coleridge's criticism, again like Burke's, is not directed against natural rights in themselves, but first against the too exclusively abstract, individual, and non-social character of the claim made in their name, and secondly against the arbitrary method of deciding what should be classified as natural rights. Locke and his disciples down to Rousseau had overlooked the fact that political thought is concerned not with an imaginary natural man, but with man as modified by and finding expression in societies. The politician must accept man as he finds him, with all the accumulated differences of social and individual development. But taken with this qualification, our common humanity, the nature we share one with another, has a claim or natural right which neither Coleridge nor Burke denied. "A natural instinct constitutes a right, as far as its gratification is compatible with the equal rights of others."(27) Legislation which runs counter to human nature is consequently not only inexpedient but morally wrong. Similarly, it is a valid criticism if laws are too good. "It is only to a limited extent that laws can be wiser than the nation for which they are enacted."(28) It is the very message of Burke.

In Coleridge we see more clearly what are the grounds of the political views which he shares with Burke. Their criticism of the utilitarians and their criticism of the rights of nature school amount to practically the same thing in the last resort. What they object to is their abstractness and their undue simplification. Helvétius and Bentham, as well as Locke, had attempted to deduce human psychology from a few first principles. Burke and Coleridge began, as far as they could, with observed facts of the mind and behaviour; scattered through Coleridge's writings are innumerable notes on mental phenomena, which almost justify Vaughan in claiming for him the title of the founder of experimental psychology. In his reference of all the sciences of man to the basic science of human nature lies the secret of Coleridge's valuable contributions to so many branches of thought. As a "subtle-souled psychologist" he has yet to come into his own: for our immediate purpose the importance of this aspect of Coleridge's mind is in its effect on his political theory. Casting Godwinism to the winds, he is led irresistibly from the individual to the social mind. "The perfect frame of a man", he writes, "is the perfect frame of a State: and in the light of this idea we must read Plato's *Republic*."(29) It follows that scientific psychological inquiry is as necessary for the study of society as for the study of the individual. So it was that Coleridge won the praise of J. S. Mill as the first to inquire "with any comprehension or depth, into the inductive laws of the existence and growth of human society".(30)

In place of a metaphysical theory of politics Coleridge adopts a scientific empiricism, and as with Burke, an empirical attitude in social psychology produces a bias in favour of conservatism. "I am firmly persuaded", he writes, "that no doctrine was ever widely diffused among various nations through successive ages and under different religions . . . which is not founded either in the nature of things or in the necessities of our nature."(31) Similarly, of course, with customs and institutions. In practice, like Burke again, he tends to forget the wide diffusion here predicated, and to bestow an undue reverence on the institutions of a single nation at a particular period. The simple fact of existence, more or less honoured by time, seems to him, as to Burke, the strongest argument that can be adduced in favour of an institution. And so, leaving natural right and utilitarianism on one side, we pass from the field of philosophy to that of history.

III

THE NATION AND THE STATE

The historic idea had been in process of development in the hey-day of the *raison raisonnante*. Coleridge, coming after the earliest pioneers, learnt the value of history—the summed experience of the race—from such writers as Lessing and Herder, still more from Burke, and most of all, perhaps, from his own poetic intuition. Alien to his own day, he found the contemporaries of his mind in past ages, and in claiming kinship with them, demonstrated the enduring life of the past in the present. In bare outline he achieved the historic idea; for him, more truly than for Bolingbroke, was it to be "Philosophy teaching by examples".(1) But we cannot accept Aynard's view that Coleridge was so much under the influence of the ideas of the past that he totally failed to understand the changes that were taking place in the present.(2) We see him on the contrary as one of the few men of his generation who really grasped the significance of the great intellectual and social metamorphosis which the Western world was undergoing, judging that precisely because, to use Hazlitt's phrase, his was a mind "reflecting ages past" he understood more fully than his contemporaries what was happening in the present.

As a matter of fact, though, just as Coleridge was not an abstract theorist in politics, so he was not essentially a theorist of the historic school, as the term is generally taken. The particular significance of his outlook lies not so much in either its historic or its philosophic aspects separately as in the manner in which they combine and temper one another. Standing midway between the eighteenth and the nineteenth centuries, he shares in and combines what are generally taken as the leading characteristics of both, uniting the analytic and rational spirit of the one to the historical spirit of the other. As a poet and as a disciple of Burke, his natural tendency was to appeal to the facts of observation, to the sensual world

178

of experience, and so to history. But as a student of the German Idealists, he had learnt to subordinate history to philosophy, and to discover in the historic process only the evolution of a philosophically conceived idea. In fact, the obvious intention of Coleridge is to make philosophy and not history the foundation of his theory of the State; but the force of the contrary tradition in English thinking—a tradition which found its full realization in Burke—is shown by the irresistible tendency of Coleridge to turn more and more to the positive facts of historical evolution. This transition is the weakest point in his whole argument. Unable either to reconcile history and philosophy in a broader view of both, or to keep them clearly apart, he falls into the common error of the idealist school by simply confusing them. Thus he begins his discussion of the British Constitution with a pseudo-philosophical statement of the "Idea" of the Constitution, a starting-point which he defends on the ground that the true constitution of a country is never realized in any of the actual systems of government it has from time to time possessed, and so cannot be discovered by studying their historic evolution. The Idea—the self-realizing theory—must first be apprehended by the pure reason and then used to reduce the observed facts to order. This is the metaphysical plan at its maddest, but fortunately Coleridge never carried the programme out, and in effect his method is sociological, basing his generalizations on the facts, and erecting constitutional theory on the observed historical trend of events. All the same, the priority his theory assigns to the philosophical element has important consequences.

The result of this interaction between the historic and the philosophic in his mind can be shown most clearly by his treatment of the theory of the social contract. He does not jettison it completely, as Hume and Bentham do, but he proceeds one stage further than Burke in relieving it of historical content. Burke had never really made up his mind whether he wanted to do without a contract theory altogether, Bentham rejected the whole theory as a stupid fiction, but Coleridge, granting it was a fiction, asked what was the fact that accounted for its wide acceptance. Speaking historically, he says of the conception of an original contract that it is "incapable of historic proof as a fact, and it is senseless as a theory"; because it implies as a condition of its making the very sense of social duty for the creation of which it is alleged to be necessary.(3) Unhampered by allegiance to any abstract theory of a state of nature, Coleridge can admit that man is essentially a social animal, from the beginning in society, that there is no state of nature, and consequently no necessity of assuming a social contract as a means of escape from such a state.

Philosophically, however, the social contract cannot be dismissed so easily. If there is any difference between political society and a band of robbers, an act of consent, he says, must be supposed on the part of the governed. Maitland criticizes Coleridge for founding political right on a supposition, but this is to misinterpret him. For him a necessary philosophic supposition is a surer foundation than a historic fact. He claims that the idea of a contract is a necessity of philosophy and of human psychology; and that whether it is embodied in any particular historic event or not is irrelevant. The essential fact is, as he sees it, that men can be governed permanently through their sense of duty and through that alone. As Rousseau puts it—and Coleridge is not in 1806 above quoting him—the

180

strongest must turn his strength into right if he would retain his dominion. He dismisses the school of Hobbes, the disciples of blood and iron, with the valid criticism that fear cannot produce a constant and calculable effect on political society. "The fear, which does act systematically upon the mind, always presupposes a sense of duty, as its cause."(4) Now this sense of duty, by which our moral relations as members of a body politic are determined, is a fact which can best be represented by the symbol of a contract. "It assuredly cannot be denied, that an original,—more accurately, an ever-originating,—contract is a very natural and significant mode of expressing the reciprocal duties of subject and sovereign."(5) Thus the great value of the contract is seen to be as a means of indicating the ethical nature of the State. The recognition of this, which lies for Coleridge at the root of all sound political speculation, implies that on the one hand the motives which uphold the political institution, and on the other the ends to which it is directed, must be good; or, as the Greek philosophers put it, that the end of the State is the good life.

It is in the light of this view that Coleridge approaches the problem of the relations of society and the individual. The end of the State being the good life for all its members, it possesses a moral right to those things necessary for the adequate fulfilment of its function, and this involves duties on the part of individuals; while on the other hand the State has its reciprocal duties towards its citizens. Rights and duties are correlative, there are no rights without corresponding duties, and only in so far as the State fulfils its duties to individuals has it a claim over them. The justification for this claim on the allegiance of the individual, to put it another way, only exists when in carrying out the will of the State the individual is following also what would be the dictates of his own reason if it were sufficiently enlightened. He has the duty of serving the ends of the State only if in those ends is to be found his true self-realization; because a thing may be used as a means to an end, but a person must always be included in the end, if the latter is to be of an ethical nature.(6)

We are now in a position to examine Coleridge's definition of the State. For him the extent to which a State approaches the ideal identification of the ends of the whole and of the individual in a moral organism is the criterion of its true statehood. He is even farther removed than Burke from the eighteenth-century conception of the State, which limited it to the idea of a body of persons situated on a definite territory and under the rule of a single political sovereign. His unwillingness to emphasize the omnipotence of the State or the legislature shows that he has realized—what some political thinkers have failed to see—the limitations of the conception of sovereignty. Used outside the law courts, he says, it is mere bombast, "an hyperbole that would contain mischief in it, were it only that it tends to provoke a detailed analysis of the materials of the joint-stock company, to which so terrific an attribute belongs, and the competence of the shareholders in this earthly omnipotence to exercise the same".(7)

In practice, English thinkers have seldom really believed in the idea of sovereignty; Locke, muddled and compromising, has always been the typical English political theorist and in some ways the wisest. But in the age of the Benevolent Despots and Napoleon and of the government of William Pitt, it was a lesson worth repeating that sovereignty is a conception really only valuable in law.

Moreover Coleridge was one of the first to denounce the theory of sovereignty in so many words, and that not because of the rival claims of any other association inside or outside the State, such as an economic or religious grouping, but because of the inherent extravagance of the conception itself. To overthrow State sovereignty and substitute for it the sovereignty of a thousand and one petty groups, as some political thinkers have attempted to do, is mere multiplication of evil. Coleridge goes on different principles. Against the Imperial and Papal theory of sovereignty, he asserts the national and Protestant principles of the individual conscience and the national consciousness, things which cannot be defined in terms of institutional sovereignties; for the State regards only classes and conditions, not individuals; whereas the nation, which does concern individuals, is not a power organization. As a moral and religious person, the individual is above the competence of sovereignty, and the pretence of the Jacobins that the State has authority over him as such is the creation of a tyranny.(8) We may add that it was also the pretence of the *ancien régime*: Coleridge's criticism is really as dangerous to the government of William Pitt as to that of Robespierre. The law, he wrote in the *Friend*, is to preserve internal tranquillity, not morality or religion, and although in *Church and State* he gave it wider scope, he never withdrew from the position that it knew nothing of moral guilt and could create only legal right.(9)

Thus Coleridge, discarding in his turn the eighteenth-century State, arrives at that idea of a national community which Burke had already come to by one route and Wordsworth by another. But it is important to note one respect in which he differs profoundly from Burke: he insists that the moral unity of the nation is a thing apart from its institutions. King and Parliament may represent the unity of the people, but the nation *is* the unity itself. He was fond of quoting George Withers' lines:

> Let not your king and parliament in *one*,
> Much less apart, mistake themselves for that
> Which is most worthy to be thought upon:
> Nor think *they* are, essentially, The STATE.
>
> .　　　　.　　　　.　　　　.
>
> But let them know, 'twas for a deeper life,
> Which they but *represent*—
> That there's on earth a yet auguster thing,
> Veil'd though it be, than parliament and king!(10)

That auguster thing he took to be the spirit of the nation: in a sense it is the voice of the people, for the voice of the people, be it *vox dei* or *vox diaboli*, is undoubtedly to Coleridge's mind a great spirit.

By his realization that there exists behind the State something which he calls the nation, Coleridge is carrying on the tradition of Burke and Wordsworth; he joins to it the newer influence of the Idealist philosophers. He takes Burke's vision of the national community, and restates it in the language of Idealism, with the nation conceived as an ideal society, by which he means a society inspired by an Idea, a self-conscious and ethically determined community. But although the terms are not quite the same there is no real difference between Burke's and Coleridge's nation. There is a difference, however, when they discuss the relation of this ideal society to the State. Here is the critical point in political philosophy, and it is in this connection that Coleridge rises superior both to Burke and to the Idealists. As we have seen, he frankly recognizes the limitations of the political institution and admits that it can never adequately represent the ideal, and so never possess in full the claims on the individual which are justly made by the Idea of the State, or as Wordsworth would say, by the Nation. German writers, he thinks, are too much awed by the actual political institution, "and thus give to Caesar what is God's".

It follows from this that Coleridge will, no more than Burke, take the State as an "organism". He defines it in *Church and State* as "synonymous with a constituted realm, kingdom, commonwealth, or nation; that is, where the integral parts, classes, or orders are so balanced, or so interdependent, as to constitute, more or less, a moral unit, an organic whole".(11) A world of judicious compromise lies in that "more or less", for, like Burke, Coleridge adopts a position intermediate between the organic and the mechanistic theories of the nature of the State. The State, he says, is "a result from, and not a mere total of, the parts, and yet not so merging the constituent parts in the result, but that the individual exists integrally within it".(12) In the *Essay on Faith*, he approaches nearer to what was to be the Hegelian position: "Unlike a million of tigers, a million of men is very different from a million times one man. Each man in a numerous society is not only co-existent with, but virtually organized into, the multitude of which he is an integral part. His *idem* is modified by the *alter*. And there arise impulses and objects from this *synthesis* of the *alter et idem*, myself and my neighbour."(13) This is to assert that man is a gregarious animal, whereas the tiger is not, and that this fact is so fundamental as virtually to orientate and govern the individual's life. Without society the individual is inconceivable; he is essentially social, and society is, therefore, "a moral unit, an organic whole". But Coleridge does not use these terms of the State without guarding himself against misinterpretation. The description of the State as a body politic seems to him a valuable and pregnant metaphor, but he warns the reader as definitely as Burke does against taking it as anything more than an analogy: it must not be construed as proof of a fact.(14)

Less active a politician, but a deeper philosopher, Coleridge continually reminds us of Burke. If the mantle of the author of the *Reflections* descended on anyone it was on the former young Pantisocrat. The political philosophy of Coleridge is that of Burke modified and developed on all sides, and, we may claim, not altogether losing in value in the process. But while Burke's teaching had been heard by fairly willing if uncomprehending ears in the early Revolutionary age, his successor found conditions greatly altered. Nineteenth-century England had no time for a philosophic Tory; it was too much concerned with making money to worry over abstract speculation, too keenly interested in the immediate future to have much feeling for the past; and so Coleridge found himself a lonely thinker, with no inspiration save in retrospect, and no hope but in reaction, hovering fitfully over the Middle Ages—who knows?—drawing life somehow from those deserted fields.

NOTES

I   1. Lett. I. 243: April, 1798.
    2. Poet. Works.
    3. E. Halévy: Histoire d'Angleterre, I. 557.
    4. Mrs. H. Sandford: T. Poole and his Friends (1888),
       II. 306.

5. Statesman's Manual, 313.
6. Friend, III. 146 n.; Statesman's Manual, 321.
7. Lay Sermon, 404.
8. Aids to Reflection, 100.

II 1. Friend, I. 265.
2. Id. I. 268.
3. Essays on His Own Times, 352.
4. Friend, I. 247.
5. MS. note in W. Godwin: Thoughts occasioned by Dr. Parr's Spital Sermon, 1801. p. 7 (Br. Mus.).
6. Essays on His Own Times, 698–700: 1814.
7. Stuart: Letters from the Lake Poets, 276–7.
8. Biographia Literaria, 104.
9. Statesman's Manual, 340.
10. Essays on His Own Times, 689.
11. Table-Talk, 107, 120, 247.
12. Id. 78, 107.
13. Friend, I. 72.
14. Lay Sermon, 392.
15. Anima Poetae, 174
16. Friend, I. 87.
17. Id. I. 232.
18. Table-Talk, 134–5; cf. Friend (first edition), p. 164; Essays on His Own Times, 654–6; Biographia Epist. 35.
19. Essays on His Own Times, 652; Church and State, 70.
20. Southey: Colloquies, II. 194–5.
21. Table-Talk, 134–5.
22. Aids to Reflection, 31.
23. Id.
24. Anima Poetae, 142.
25. F. H. Bradley: Ethical Studies, 250.
26. Literary Remains, I. 382.
27. Church and State, 75–6.
28. Id. 163.
29. Statesman's Manual, 340.
30. J. S. Mill: Dissertations and Discussions, I. 425.
31. Literary Remains, I. 322–3.

III   1. Cf. Statesman's Manual, 312.

2. Aynard: La Vie d'un Poète: Coleridge (1907), 355.

3. Church and State, 15; Friend, I. 228.

4. Friend, I. 219, 225, 227; first edition, 106.

5. Friend, I. 229; cf. Church and State, 15.

6. Church and State, 15; Friend, I. 254.

7. Church and State, 103–5.

8. Lett. 635; Table-Talk, 107.

9. Friend, I. 115; Stuart, op. cit. 249.

10. Table-Talk, 119.

11. Church and State, 117.

12. Table-Talk, 146.

13. Aids to Reflection, 347.

14. Church and State, 90.

CHAPTER VII

THE LAKE POETS AND SOCIAL REFORM

I

ECONOMIC IDEAS OF BURKE

WITH COLERIDGE the development of Romantic political theory in England comes to a sudden halt. The Romantic poets of the second generation, headed by Shelley and Byron, belong to quite another tradition: so far as their political ideas are concerned they are disciples of the eighteenth century. Burke, Wordsworth, and Coleridge thus form an isolated group, the broader significance of which we must leave to the concluding chapter. Meanwhile, however, it is obvious that the link which unites them, and distinguishes them from orthodox eighteenth- and nineteenth-century political thinkers, is their theory of the nature of the national community. In Burke we see the idea still struggling in the toils of the Lockian State; Wordsworth exhibits it in its international consequences; and Coleridge attempts to draw out of it a restatement of the basis of political life and of the relations of the State and the nation. But strict political theory by no means exhausts the significance of their new view of society, though little attention has been paid to its other aspects. Perhaps the field in which the successors of Burke expended their greatest energies is precisely that in which the least effort has been made since to reap the fruits of their thought. Burke's works will, of course, for long remain the *vade mecum* of statesmen and the school of political wisdom; the *Convention of Cintra* is still read and provides a useful corrective of modern exaggerated views of nationalism; while Coleridge's criticism of democracy is hardly novel to the present day. When, however, we turn to the writings, particularly of Coleridge and Southey, on social questions, we find that their ideas evoked a very inadequate response from their own generation, and that to-day, while hardly less appropriate than a hundred years ago, they are almost completely forgotten.

The Lake Poets are treated generally, though as previous chapters indicate, not altogether justly, as the spokesmen of extreme Toryism. As far as their political ideas are concerned there is at any rate a semblance of plausibility in this view, though the necessary qualifications will be at once obvious; but in their dealing with economic questions the true originality of their theory of society appears. In order, however, adequately to appreciate this, it is necessary to say something of the prevailing outlook. There is no need to seek far, since Burke himself will provide us with an example of the orthodox economic creed. His views are all the more indicative of its strength inasmuch as they are based on principles entirely opposed to those which his political thought more and more tended to adopt.

At first sight one might suppose Burke's economic theories to be quite in keeping with his political. What is more prescriptive than property? Burke is going no farther than common opinion in maintaining that the principles regulating economic relations and the distribution of wealth were established directly by God, and consequently that interference with these is sacrilegious and not to be thought of. Economic laws, he writes—the laws of commerce—are the laws of nature, that is, the laws of God. It is curious to see how Burke, in true eighteenth-century fashion, confers a divine halo on the principle of utility; for this is the true justification of his statement, and if the axiom that the laws of commerce are the laws of God sounds strange in our ears, we may restate it thus: obedience to the rules which determine commercial prosperity is a condition of the public well-being, and since it is the desire of God that His people should be happy, the laws conditioning that end may be taken as divinely decreed. The problem of the eighteenth century, as we saw in the first chapter, was: What are these laws? Burke is amongst those who attempt an answer, though not in so many words.

His actual writings on economic theory amount to only a few pages, but very revealing they are, for all their brevity. He had researched into the facts of economic life with considerable perseverance, more thoroughly than was necessary merely to construct the platitudinous generalizations with which the economic writings of the eighteenth and nineteenth centuries are too liberally punctuated; though the only work in which he specifically deals with questions of economic theory is the *Thoughts and Details on Scarcity*, 1795, the object of which was to prove to Pitt that the Government's efforts to relieve the distresses of the poor were futile and unnecessary. The strength of Burke's feelings may be judged by the violent terms of a letter of the following year. "In the name of God, what is the meaning of this project of Mr. Pitt concerning the further relief of the Poor? What relief do they want, except that which it will be difficult indeed to give, to make them more frugal or more industrious? I see he's running for popular plates with Mr. Fox."(1)

Burke considers the condition of the "labouring poor" greatly meliorated in the present age. True, they work harder, but then they fare better. Labour is after all "the common doom of man", and they are men like ourselves and perhaps all the happier for having no resource but their own hands and the gifts all men receive from nature. Their pleasures are different from those of the rich, but not therefore inferior. Have they not—greatest of blessings—the heaven-sent gift of gin? The Divine wisdom has appointed the poor their place in the world, and they must accept it with thankful hearts, finding their consolation in the proportions of eternal justice, and meanwhile cherishing "patience, labour, sobriety, frugality, and religion."

Government, declares Burke, must not attempt to supply that which nature has withheld: it has neither the duty nor the power of providing the necessities of life for the people. Labour is a commodity and its price is subject to the natural laws of trade. And of these the first is the principle whereby every man seeks his own interest. Burke thoughtfully acknowledges the authority of "the benign and wise Disposer of all things, who obliges men, whether they will or not, in pursuing their own selfish interests, to connect the general good with their own individual success".(2) In other words, he adopts the passive and conservative principle of the necessary identification of the interests of the individual and society by nature, rather than the active and reforming idea that the reconciliation is to be assisted artificially by the operation of government. It follows that government—comfortable doctrine—can do nothing to alleviate the distresses of the poor. On the contrary it is the people who out of the superfluity of their produce maintain their governors and indeed all the rich—pensioners of the poor, he even calls them. It was left for Coleridge to follow up that point, however; Burke does not draw from it any ethical obligation beyond the ordinary religious duty of occasional charity, though it is only fair to remember how generously he himself fulfilled that duty. Perhaps he thought others equalled his own benevolence. The amount and manner of its exercise is, at all events, to be determined by private discretion; government has no function in this connection.

From *laissez-faire* it is natural to turn to *laissez-passer*— the less governments meddle with trade the better: commerce, like labour, must be left to itself, for Burke is one of the first prophets of free trade. Indeed, Adam Smith is alleged to have told him that he was the only man who without previous communications had proved to hold the same views on economic subjects as he himself did. "It is the interest of the commercial world that wealth should be found everywhere", Burke wrote to his constituents of Bristol, defending his support of the freeing of the Irish trade. Besides this valuable but unpopular step, he took a leading part in the abolition of the old mediaeval statutes against forestallers and regrators in 1772.

Behind the principles of free trade and laissez-faire which Burke thus accepts as the basis of economic life, is one even more sacred. It needs no saying that for Burke property is the foundation of society. "Too much and too little is treason against property." He talks of it just as though it were one of those abstract rights he is elsewhere so fond of abusing, but the sophistries of Locke are not sufficient justification of property for him. When he is expressing his own ideas and not merely repeating jargon, he justifies property on the ground of prescription, and so comes to the principle nearest his heart. Not only from its origin, but also for its consequences is the institution of property to be revered. Government, as Locke had shown, was established for its protection. Attack property and you attack government; destroy property and you destroy civil society; nay, law, religion, and morality will fall in its train. His detestation of French atheism and disloyalty may be more furious, it can scarcely be more deep-rooted than his indignation at the wickedness of the treatment meted out to the landed aristocracy by the revolutionaries. The application of the Rights of Man to property, he declared in a speech of 1792, "caused most of the horrors of the French Revolution". The report preserves for us the "Hear, hear!" evoked by that sentiment. Nothing is so fatal to property, he holds, as equality and popular sovereignty. It is unjust to extend the privileges of citizenship to the man who does not help to support the community by paying taxes; it is fatal to extend them to the man who has no interest in the maintenance of the laws of property. Give the formation of government to the "no-property people", and they will first of all plunder the rich and then turn and rend one another. Here was the original fault in the Revolution, and until it had been remedied, until property had been restored to its old order and allowed to form a government agreeable to itself, no negotiations should be entered into with France. If on one side the war against Jacobinism is a war between atheism and Christianity, on another it is the conflict of property and force—a class war on a worldwide front, from which no country can hope to remain immune. Until property in France is restored, he declares, property in England is not worth a ten years' purchase.

The especial duty of Parliamentary representatives is to safeguard the property of those they represent, the Whig theory being, as we have already explained, that men of property are the country's natural legislators, because their interests are the public's. Burke emphasizes the importance of representing property in large masses; he argues, rather illogically, that the diffusion of property weakens the system, and reaches something like absurdity in the position, surely untenable even from his own standpoint, that the more unequal property is, the better, the safer for the permanence of the institution. Again, the richer a capitalist is, the less profit in proportion need he take, and consequently the richer he is the more closely his interests correspond with those of the public. This is mere special pleading. But we must not forget that Burke naturally thinks in terms of landed property and regards the majority of a country's landowners as being in a middling way, clustering round and protected by a few great proprietors.(3) In his time the problem of vast accumulations of capital had not dawned on the economic horizon, while the English agricultural labourer was enjoying one of the most prosperous periods he has ever known.

In Burke's undergraduate days property had overawed him less: it had seemed to him primarily a trust. "Our modern Systems hold", he wrote in the *Reformer*, "that the Riches and Power of Kings are by no means their Property, but a Depositum in their Hands, for the Use of the People: And if we consider the natural Equality of Mankind, we shall believe the same of the Estates of Gentlemen, bestowed on them at the first distribution of Properties for promoting the Public Good."(4) Coleridge makes great play with the same idea later, and

in view of the admirable manner in which it would fit
into Burke's political system it is surprising that he never
recurs to it. Perhaps that is because he takes it so completely
for granted that the propertied classes do as a matter of
course fulfil all their duties. "Burke", Acton said, "had
no conception of the evils of class government, being a
defender of antiquity."(5) This would seem to be true
enough in general, but we must remember that in the
Vindication of Natural Society he has described very
rhetorically the social division into rich and poor, the
poor ministering to the follies of the rich, the latter in
return enslaving them the worse. True this was satire,
but that production of his rash youth, the *Reformer*,
contains an even more highly coloured picture of the
startling antithesis presented by the misery and luxury
of different classes.(6) It would be truer then to say that
he chose not to see this aspect of social life than that he
was incapable of seeing it.

His conservative political instincts, his aristocratic
associations, his religious ideas, the Lockian doctrine of
property, the theories of Adam Smith and the Physiocrats, all combined to dictate his economic modes of
thought. Summed up in the principles of free trade,
laissez-faire and the inalienable right of private property,
they are based on natural right and unqualified individualism: which means that they are utterly alien from what
we have seen to be the increasing trend of his political
ideas. His economic views are the culmination of Lockian
Whiggism of the eighteenth century and a foreshadowing
of the classical economy of the nineteenth at its worst:
they show to what extremes a naturally benevolent
statesman could be led by theory. On the whole it was
as well for his future reputation that Burke produced

only one economic pamphlet, for on no other subject are both the limitations and the excesses of his mind so apparent.

II

MEDIAEVALISM, RELIGION AND ECONOMICS

Such was the social outlook of the first of Romantic political thinkers, and we are compelled to ask why his successors differed in this respect not only from him but also from the vast majority of their contemporaries. The explanation is to be found in a study of certain influences to which they were subjected, of which we may take first the mediaeval revival. In the sphere of economic relations the very backward-turning mentality and reactionary sentiments of the Lake Poets enabled them to reach a position not to be attained by the social conscience for another century. For, looking back on the Middle Ages, the Romantic poets discovered a society based on principles very different from those of their own day, and as they compared what they read about the life of the mediaeval community with what they knew of modern social conditions, it seemed to them that something of value had been lost with the disappearance of feudalism. The barest traces of the mediaeval revival are to be found in Burke, though its kinship with the profoundest and most original of his ideas on the State is evident. Coleridge, Wordsworth, Scott, Southey, and others bear witness to the same trend of thought. Not the least interesting of those who idealized the Middle Ages was William Cobbett. Although the supposed virtues of mediaeval barons and monks were certainly useful to hold up in comparison with the failings of later possessors of the soil—the Establishment and the squirearchy—his sincerity in this matter cannot be questioned. It would be a work of supererogation to elaborate on Cobbett's mediaevalism. His books are crowded with appeals to the good old days and denunciations of the new-rich of the Napoleonic wars. What have the people gained, he asks, by the fall of the feudal system? "Talk of *vassals*! Talk of *villains*! Talk of *serfs*! Are there any of these, or did feudal times ever see any of them, so debased, so absolutely slaves, as the poor creatures who, in the 'enlightened' north, are compelled to work fourteen hours in a day, in a heat of eighty-four degrees; and who are liable to punishment for looking out at a window of the factory!"(1)

Southey, the historian, is naturally the most conspicuous figure amongst those who shared in this particular orientation of the mediaeval revival. He wrote his *Colloquies with Sir Thomas More* for the specific purpose of putting into comparison mediaeval and modern ideas about society. Whereas mediaeval society was based on the recognition of the interdependence of its members, the essence of modern social relationships seemed to him to be found in personal independence, for which a heavy price was paid in the loss of "kindly feelings and ennobling attachments". "It is no advantage",. he writes, "for anyone to possess that sort of independence which consists in not being subject to the rules of a decent family."(2) Wordsworth also laments the rupture of those feudal ties that had kept the classes in "harmonious interdependence". Take, again, Southey's description of the old landowner: "The representative of an old family, who resides on the lands of his ancestors,

198

and sees around him their portraits in his mansion, and their tombs in his parish church, is surrounded by hereditary attachments; he succeeds to their principles and feelings and duties as part of his inheritance, not less than to their honours and their wealth . . . the old tenants are as precious to him as the old trees on his estate, and the domestics have, as the name ought to imply, their home and resting-place in his service". The writer sadly ends, "There is little of this remaining in England".(3)

A second source of altered views on society lay in a transformation of the religious atmosphere, a religious revival, which in many cases was turned to the service of the new industrial system, but which with a few thinkers resulted in a changed attitude towards social problems. Coleridge's religion harked back to early days. He took the Lutheran teaching of the self-sufficiency in faith of the individual soul and combined with it the social ideals of mediaeval Christendom. From the Revolution he had learnt the rights of man; religion restated the lesson for him in terms of duties. This is to put religion to a very different use from that made of it by most of his contemporaries. It is worth while reminding ourselves how little exalted was the eighteenth-century theory of the uses of religion by a quotation from the worthy and generous-minded Wilberforce. Of the Christian religion he writes, "Softening the glare of wealth, and moderating the insolence of power, she renders the inequalities of the social state less galling to the lower orders, whom also she instructs in their turn, to be diligent, humble, and patient: reminding them that their more lowly path has been allotted to them by the hand of God; . . . that the present state of things is very short; . . . finally, that all human distinctions will soon be done away. . . . Such

199

are the blessed effects of Christianity on the temporal well-being of political communities."(4) This expresses in moderate language the view of the Established Church. Similarly Methodism, under the conservative influence of Wesley, was accustomed to recommend itself to authority as a useful supplement to the police force.

We said it was an unexalted conception of religion, but although liable in the minds of sceptics like Gibbon and Horace Walpole to become mere cynicism, although apt even in the best to be a tattered cloak for self-interest, Christianity did at any rate give society the sanctity required in one form or another if social obligations were to be duly honoured. Nor is the result essentially deadening and reactionary, if easily bent in that direction. What matters in the long run is its essential principle as distinguished from the accretions of prejudice and self-interest. It made society divine and yet not omnipotent, sacred and yet not incapable of improvement. It conferred on the community a religious ordination, but only in so far as it was faithful to a religious end. Now the moral and spiritual welfare of the individual was undeniably part of this end; the physical welfare not so obviously, but even the latter might be derived by thinkers who pushed their arguments far enough. The welfare of the individual was also the fundamental object of utilitarianism, which thus during the eighteenth century became mixed up with Providence. Burke had argued that, the happiness of His people being the undoubted wish of God, if society is to claim a divine sanction it must be as working towards that end. But he assumed that, apart from the occasional misdeeds of Tories or democrats, society did in fact perform all that it could or should in this direction.

The poets of romanticism were more critical and their

ideals less static. The progressive faith they had learned
from Godwin and the Revolutionary thinkers was carried
over into Toryism. From founding their hopes on *Political
Justice* they came to found them on the Bible—the "Statesman's Manual" for Coleridge, "the clear annunciation of
that kingdom of God upon earth",(5) for Southey. "As
surely as God is good", wrote the latter, careless of heresy,
"so surely there is no such thing as necessary evil."(6)
The observations of the Lake Poets may more often seem
to differ little from the customary pious platitudes of
eighteenth-century churchmen; the difference is in the
application. Orthodox divines were giving Tory reaction
a lengthened lease of life by the concoction of soporifics
for the poor: their religion was a Pangloss philosophy.
Southey and Coleridge were preparing the way for
reform by a religion which was a call to every class in the
name of social progress.

Religion and mediaevalism combined to teach the Romantic poets the social responsibilities of property and
power. From the Middle Ages they learnt that society is
a whole greater than any of its parts, that the interest of
the community is greater than that of any separate class
and is the main end to be sought. They were saved
from an excessive worship of the State, on the other
hand, by religion, which taught the value and uniqueness
of individual life. It followed that the claims of each individual as a moral person should predominate over everything except corresponding claims in others. Thus social
institutions only possessed validity in so far as they
fulfilled the moral personality of the individuals forming
society. Here came in the opportunity to draw a practical
conclusion, because unfortunately we know by experience
that there is a persistent tendency for institutions to

attract to themselves the loyalty that belongs rightly only
to the end for which they exist, a tendency which is
accentuated by the linking of institutions with the interests
of some section of the community as opposed to the
remainder. Thus in the eighteenth and nineteenth centuries the absolute rights of private property had come to
possess in and for themselves and apart entirely from
fulfilment of function a sacrosanct character such as they
had never had before. It was against this aberration
that the Lake Poets protested, and in support of their
protest appealed to the disappearing religious ideals of
earlier ages.

Coleridge in particular was insistent on the need for
reviving "the idea of a *trust* inherent in landed property".
During the Middle Ages, he points out, the possession of
property without duties correspondent thereto was the
mark of non-membership of the community, of the alien
and the Jew.(7) According to him the "idea" of our law
of real estate, as distinguished from the law of personal
property, is fiduciary. Maitland makes the criticism that
on the contrary the tendency which began in the Middle
Ages and has continued ever since has been to approxi-
mate increasingly the law of realty to the law of person-
alty,(8) and that hence Coleridge's theory of our law is
the reverse of its predominate tendency. He knew this
himself: originally confined to movables, the notion of
personal property, he agreed, had received an unfortunate
extension. Because money and stock have not such
evident responsibilities going with their ownership as has
land, ideas of absolute property rights had grown up in
connection with them in an age when personal property
was comparatively unimportant. These ideas, he admits,
have been retained, although real estate is becoming an

202

increasingly small proportion of the wealth of the country, and have even spread to property in land.(9) But this tendency does not in his eyes affect the fact that in an ideal scheme property should be treated as a social institution, and held as a trust.

Even if they had gone no farther it was a great revolution in ideas when Coleridge and his friends began to talk not about the rights of property but about its social duties, to criticize the economic operation of individualism from the point of view of the whole community, and to suggest that the State had sometimes the duty of interfering in economic matters and even of limiting unrestricted rights of property. For the absolute rights of property, strict individualism, and the exclusion of the State from the economic sphere were the three fundamental dogmas of orthodox economy. It was because he refused to accept these principles as axiomatic that Coleridge was summed up by the young Mill as in political economy an "arrant driveller".(10) Maitland, on the other hand, thought that some of the deductions of economists both of his own day and of Coleridge's went far to justify the latter's characterization of political economy as "solemn humbug". Economics, according to Coleridge, was an abstract study, with abstract conclusions, which could never be reduced to practice; it excluded all human nature not subject to technical calculation, but treated the remainder as if it were the whole.(11) Even if the first process were possible, the second was illegitimate, because it resulted in an abstract entity, or rather non-entity, which the economists called the economic man, being set up in place of the real man and becoming an idol in the name of which human happiness was ruthlessly sacrificed.(12) The same complaint comes from Southey, that economists do not treat of the real man at all: their basic conceptions, he says, are the economic man and the self-interest principle, ideas hardly more absurd than they are wicked. The economists' doctrines, Coleridge concludes, are simply a cover for the self-interest of the rich, to be ignored whenever it suits their purpose.(13).

The economist Coleridge comes most violently into conflict with is Malthus. He is the only anti-Malthusian of the period who need be taken very seriously, for Southey's attack in the *Annual Review* is an almost word for word reproduction of Coleridge's notes on the copy of the *Essay on Population* now in the British Museum. The two poets belabour Malthus with zest: his doctrine is termed a pandering to the cruelty and avarice of men. Although the edition annotated is the second, into which Malthus had introduced the check of moral restraint, Southey still indicts him with putting hunger and lust on the same level as physical necessities.(14) The pseudo-religious argument finds its place. Population must inevitably increase; it is the law of nature, and therefore the law of Providence, which has assuredly made the earth "capacious enough for all the creatures whom it was intended to support". To attempt artificially to interfere with the natural and divinely ordained multiplication of man is an abominable crime against God. But of course, "moral restraint" is an excellent thing, and the lower fecundity of the upper classes indicates an admirable prudence.(15)

Coleridge put the matter on a more rational basis than Southey. In particular there is one note which we must quote at length. "If we believed with Mr. Malthus's *warmest* partisans that man will never in general be capable of regulating the sexual appetite by the Law of Reason, and that the gratification of Lust is a thing of physical necessity equally with the gratification of Hunger—a faith which we should laugh at for its silliness if its wickedness had not pre-excited abhorrence—nothing could be more easy than to demonstrate, that some one or other of these actions, whether Abortion, or the Exposure of Children, or artificial sterility on the part of the Male, would become Virtues—a thought which we turn from with loathing; but not with greater Loathing, than we do from the degrading Theory, of which it would be a legitimate consequences (*sic*)—and which by a strange Inconsequence admits the existence of all these Vices, and of all that mass of Misery on account of which alone these Vices are Vices, in order to prevent that State of Society, in which admitting some one of these actions after the birth of the second or third Child, the whole earth might be imagined filled to its utmost extent with enlightened and happy Beings. Mr. Malthus is continually involving himself in the silly blunder of the Quakers, who idolize words.''(16) Coleridge's own view would perhaps not be accepted by many to-day, but he has certainly hit upon the chief weakness of Malthus's argument. He seems to mean that if we accept the premises of Malthus some form of birth control would become a social virtue, and that in preferring to this the mass of war, disease, vice, and misery which form the existing checks on population, Malthus is illogical, because he is preferring the greater ill to the less. Coleridge himself refuses to admit the necessity for either alternative.

To return to the general argument, the fact was that the economists had vitiated their study for practical purposes by a tendency to disregard all but material results and at the same time to treat their conclusions as final and all-embracing. Typical of the eighteenth century in their outlook, they claimed to have built up a system of laws as immutable as the laws of physical science were supposed to be. It is possible to trace in their attitude, first a misconception of the nature of scientific law, and then a further confusion with the legal view of law as a command. The greater founders of economics had a truer idea of the limitations of their study, but many of their disciples were apt to speak in the magistral tones of the prophets of a new religion. If they had been willing to enter on their task in a humbler spirit and had paid more heed to their critics, some at least of the evil that followed in their train might have been averted. In effect they tried to turn a science dealing with certain means useful towards the attainment of the good life into a philosophy of ends. "The system which produces the happiest moral effects", wrote Southey, indicating the true direction of argument, "will be found also most beneficial to the interest of the individual and to the general weal: upon this basis the science of political economy will rest at last."(17)

III

A PROTEST AGAINST THE INDUSTRIAL SYSTEM

By now the theoretical reasons for the abandonment of the economic outlook represented by Burke should be sufficiently elaborated. Mediaevalism, the religious revival, and Burke's own anti-individualistic political theory each played its part. In practice also, the lesson was underlined by the industrial developments of the early nineteenth century, by conditions which perhaps were not worse than they had been under the domestic system, but which being more concentrated and on a larger scale, struck more acutely on an awakening social conscience, and—above all—which were driven home by an ever-present fear of Jacobinism, class war, and social revolution. As a result of this development the State was compelled most reluctantly to re-enter the economic sphere, from which as far as possible eighteenth-century theorists and politicians had tried to exclude it.

The views of the Lake Poets showed considerable insight into the nature and potentialities of the State as an economic society, though they were far in advance both of the general ideas and of the facts of the time. They and their opponents fell into opposite errors. The economists assumed that because existing governments were for the most part hopelessly inefficient, therefore no government should ever interfere in the economic life of the nation. Coleridge and Southey assumed that because ideally a State should be capable of useful action even in economic matters, therefore the economic functioning of all States was to be deemed beneficent. Perhaps it was necessary that the negative work of the economists should be done before the positive building up could take place. It is none the less regrettable that social ideals such as Coleridge and Southey put forward should have been either ignored or else ridiculed until the extreme individualist school had finally worked itself out to a self-contradiction. Even in the hey-day of industrial change, when maximum freedom was needed, it was not wrong to trace much evil to the influence of rigid laissez-faire doctrines, although in existing conditions of administration any attempt at State interference must necessarily have been inadequate.

What was worst in the contemporary outlook was the passive acceptance of social evils as the inevitable outcome of human nature and economic law. The romanticists on the contrary carried over the belief in social progress that had inspired their youth into their Tory period; the Sermon on the Mount reinforced the lessons of *Political Justice*. They did not believe that human nature was evil, and if the fault for so much misery and crime was not in human nature, then it must be in the arrangements of society. "We are", said Southey, applying an idea borrowed from the *philosophes*, "in great degree, what our institutions make us." Now the most apparent evil in society in the early decades of the nineteenth century was the miserable conditions of the people, and this, Southey held, must be a consequence of the social system, and not, as Burke would have said, a necessity of social life.(1) Coleridge went farther and attributed the increase in pauperism directly to the new industrial system, which, he said, requires a large supply of cheap labour; virtually it calls into being a large industrial population, but refuses to accept any responsibility for its permanent maintenance. On the other hand, it subjects its workers to alternating periods of dire poverty and comparative plenty which serve equally for their demoralization. This constantly recurring unemployment produces a perpetual sense of insecurity.(2) The temporary unemployment caused by improvements in processes and the entry of women and children into industry on a large scale, on which contemporary attention concentrated, was comparatively trivial. The important phenomenon which Southey and Coleridge had discovered was not

208

this but the periodic unemployment resulting from the operation of what was to be known later as the trade cycle. Southey gives a precise description of it. In times of boom, he says, there is reckless over-production, markets are flooded with goods, and labour is at a premium; sooner or later a reaction sets in, manufactured articles can find no more buyers, a period of bad trade ensues, men are thrown out of employment on all sides, and "every return of this cold fit is more violent than the former". Scott comes in here, curiously enough, to draw the moral of taxing manufacturers for the support of the unemployed. "I cannot but think", he argues, "that the necessity of making some fund beforehand, for the provision of those whom they debauch, and render only fit for the alms-house . . . though it operated as a check on the increase of manufactures, would be a measure just in itself, and beneficial to the community." He adds, "It would never be listened to".(3)

The consequence is that society has to do the best it can by means of poor laws. This is Coleridge's reply to the Malthusian attack on the Poor Law. Southey has an even more pertinent observation on this question. "What does this precious philosopher say to Ireland, where there are no poor laws?"(4) Wordsworth in a Preface to the Poetical Works of 1835, a date by which he might have been supposed to have shed all his earlier liberal ideas, enters into an elaborate defence of the principle of poor relief. His argument is, in brief, that the individual's right of self-preservation is limited only by the same right in others. Consequently the individual is in the last extremity entitled to help himself even at the expense of other people's property, and to prevent this from occurring the Government makes provision for him. Or, if this is too dangerous a doctrine, still, does not the State stand *in loco parentis* to its subjects? And do not its claims on their allegiance imply the duty of preserving them from ruin?(5) Discreetly applied, Wordsworth held, poor relief can save the character of the working classes; it rescues men from dependence on casual charity, from despair and crime, from starvation and death.(6) To some extent, of course, the critics and defenders of the Poor Laws were arguing at cross purposes, as the former were attacking primarily outdoor relief, and the latter were quite willing to admit the desirability of reforms in their administration. Coleridge himself in his *Lay Sermon* pointed out that the chief weakness was the pauperization of the agricultural labourer by making up wages out of rates. Again Southey, "The mischief which the poor laws produce has arisen wholly from their mal-administration or perversion; the system itself is humane, just, necessary, befitting a Christian state, and honourable to the English nation".(7)

On another ground also Southey and Coleridge were opposed to the agitation against the poor laws. They were differentiated from their contemporaries by the unpopular belief that a high rate of taxation forms a natural and healthy feature of natural economy. "National wealth", they thought, "is wholesome only when it is equitably diffused",(8) and taxation, in particular a well graduated property tax, seemed to them a legitimate method of securing this more equal distribution. How revolutionary this suggestion was is shown by the general estimation of the income tax, that new and bitterly resented war-time expedient, which chancellors were to hold out hopes of abolishing for another half-century yet, and by the not altogether unreasonable national demand for economy that followed the war. Southey, on the other hand, believed that the sudden diminution in national expenditure was itself one of the chief causes of existing difficulties. But even apart from that argument he believed in the justice of a high rate of taxation. "A State cannot have more wealth at its command than may be employed for the general good, a liberal expenditure in national works being one of the surest means for promoting national prosperity, and the benefit being still more evident of an expenditure directed to the purposes of national improvement."(9) He compares taxation to the process of evaporation and rain; what is taken from the people is returned to it in a more socially useful form.(10) The Government sucks up the capital accumulated by individuals and diffuses it in health-giving showers over the whole nation. Within limits this is a correct description of the possible operation of an extremely enlightened system of taxation. But where they were mistaken, and what led to their views on taxation being, as they thought, grossly misrepresented, was in the assumption that the existing system was really beneficial in this way. They forgot that the gain to a nation from governmental expenditure would necessarily depend on the objects of that expenditure, and that the biggest calls on the Treasury of the day were for naval and military expenditure and for debt services. This mistake largely invalidated their arguments against retrenchment.

Turning from this optimistic theory of the value of taxation to the views of Coleridge on other branches of the national economy, we find that he has much to say of the justice of State interference in two particular fields. The branch to which he thought most injury was being done by an unrestricted application of individualist commercial principles was agriculture, which required principles, he alleged, essentially different from those of trade; and seemed to him of far greater importance than any industry inasmuch as its interests were far more closely identified with the interests of the State. One must remember that England was still mainly an agricultural country in the early nineteenth century, and that the old theory of the self-sufficient State, tending to die out before the growth of a large industrial population and a manufacturing interest with a rapidly growing foreign trade, had been given a new lease of life by the experience of the Napoleonic War. On this account, as well as for the maintenance of war rents and prices, the agricultural depression which followed on the peace caused alarm. It was met by a revised and prohibitive duty on corn, against which Coleridge was instrumental in getting up a local petition: he opposed it because he did not think the numerous ills from which agriculture suffered could be cured by a single crude remedy of this kind.(11) At the same time, he shared the common opinion, for which *prima facie* the case was strong, that English safety required independence of foreign corn supplies, that in the necessities of life a State should be self-sufficient, and that consequently these could not be left at the mercy of the ordinary chances of trade.(12) An added consideration was that the agricultural population is an essential element in the nation; it was still customary to regard the country gentry and the peasantry as the backbone of the nation. By the introduction of commercial methods, said Coleridge, the one has been rendered as extinct as the dodo, at any rate completely dis-rusticated, and the other reduced to a condition of pauperism or else driven right off the land.(13) Still more fatal, thought Southey, was the decay of small farmers, those yeomen who by the progress of agriculture had been reduced to the condition of day-labourers or else had fled the land altogether. The extent and time of this change is still a matter of controversy, but there are too many contemporary witnesses for us to discount it entirely. Moreover, the Lake Poets had immediately under their eyes the example of the "statesmen" in the Dales, who were rapidly losing their time-honoured rank and ancient lands, and in the course of the next half-century were almost completely to vanish. A measure of practical reform put forward by Southey was for the Government to purchase tracts of uncultivated land to be held as "national domains", and colonized with disbanded soldiers and sailors and the unemployed; if these can raise sufficient food for their own sustenance instead of being dependent on public assistance, that is sufficient profit for the State, he argues.(14) The strict economic argument against the subsidization of uneconomic labour is unanswerable; but so also is Southey's that poverty and starvation cannot be accepted as necessary incidents of social life, while large areas of fertile land remain uncultivated.

In his reflections on agriculture Coleridge had kept in mind mainly social interests; in his other demand for interference by the Government he takes up his stand on individual rights. His championship of the cause of factory children was an interesting result of his belief in the sanctity of individuality, and the right of the individual in a civilized community to a certain minimum standard of civilized existence. Making all allowances for the by no means idyllic conditions existing under the domestic system, it still remains true that the exploitation of child labour under the most appalling conditions is one of the darkest pages in the history of the industrial revolution. Coleridge says that he had been "an eye-witness of the direful effects", and that they had "weighed on his feelings from earliest manhood".(15) "Nothing so bad", writes his friend Southey, "was ever brought to light before. The slave trade is mercy to it." Yet Pitt could congratulate Parliament "that the nation had a new source of wealth and revenue in the labour of children".(16)

Comparatively recently it has been discovered that Coleridge took an active part in the agitation on behalf of Peel's Factory Children Bill of 1818. His description in one of his letters of an extraordinarily stupid speech by the Earl of Lauderdale deserves to be recalled. "Whether some half-score of rich capitalists are to be prevented from suborning suicide and perpetuating infanticide and soul-murder is, forsooth, the most perplexing question which has ever called forth his *determining* faculties."(17) But then Coleridge was ignorant of the vast economic principles at stake! He writes, rather pathetically, to Crabb Robinson: "Another mendicant letter from S.T.C.! But no, it is for the poor little children employed in Cotton Factories, who would fain have you in the list of their friends and helpers. . . . Can you furnish us with any other instances in which the Legislature has . . . interfered with what is ironically called 'free labour'? (i.e. DARED to prohibit soul-murder and infanticide on the part of the rich, and self-slaughter on that of the poor!)"(18) This information was obviously required to assist him in the composition of two tracts which have now been recovered. In these he deals very effectively with objections to the Bill.

To the argument that interference with free labour and property was illegitimate he replies that the Statute Book is crowded with proofs to the contrary. As for its being free labour, "In what sense, not utterly sophistical, can the labour of children, extorted from the wants of their parents, 'their poverty, but not their will consenting', be called free?" He goes to the root of the matter and exposes the fallacy in the arguments against factory reform. "If the labourer were indeed free, the employer would purchase, and the labourer sell, what the former had no right to buy, and the latter no right to dispose of; namely, the labourer's health, life and well-being." To the argument that the Bill would provide a dangerous precedent and that it would rouse vain hopes in the people, he replied that if the new claims anticipated were just they should be conceded, if not, the passing of the Bill could not affect them. Finally, to optimists who professed to expect reform from the humane spirit of the age through the voluntary action of manufacturers, he opposed the notorious fact of the growth of the evil. Was the Slave Trade, he asks, abolished by "the increasing humanity, the enlightened self-interests, of the slave owners?" Precisely the same objections had been brought forward in that case, to which he appeals as a glorious precedent. He wished the factory agitation to take the same lines. But though the Bill was carried, the public conscience, lulled by commercial interest and economic dogma, remained apathetic for many a year to the crying evils of industrial England.(19)

Of all the Tory reformers in the early years of the nineteenth century none was so fecund of schemes, and often sound schemes, for improving the lot of the people as Robert Southey. He often seems to us cold and unat-

tractive, but for his life of hard work, his unflinching
honour, and his practical pity for the unfortunate he
deserves a sympathetic understanding which is more
often given to frailer brethren of the pen. Among the
numerous reforms which he put forward the most prominent place was taken by emigration. It is too often forgotten that schemes of assisted emigration were an integral
part of the poor law at this period, as well as of the
criminal code. To Southey it seemed "a sure remedy for
poverty and over-population". Again and again he advo-
cates organized emigration as a permanent branch of
our national polity;(20) nor must we underestimate the
courage and insight in this proposal, although we may
know from experience that the hope it embodied is
illusory. No scheme of emigration on any practicable
scale could have hoped to cope with the annual increase
of population. Statistics show that the by no means
negligible quantity of emigration in the nineteenth century
had no appreciable effect on the growth of population in
Great Britain. Ireland presented quite a different problem. Southey's ideas are really more important from
the point of view of the new countries. He exhibits the
folly of populating them with convicts, though claiming
that the State has the right to send out paupers in place
of supporting them at home.(21) But also he wishes to see
a better class of immigrant going from choice as well as
from necessity. "It is time that Britain should become
the hive of nations, and cast her swarms; and here are
lands to receive them."(22) His amazingly modern
attitude on the question of the colonies shows that
Southey had entirely shed both the old Tory conception
of them as existing solely for the benefit of the Mother
Country, and the newer attitude which regarded them

as fruits that fall from the tree when they are ripe. Nearly twenty years after he had written thus Disraeli could say, "These wretched Colonies will all be independent in a few years, and are a mill-stone round our necks". Southey's view is that as the Mother Country withdraws her tutelage the relation of dependence will be succeeded by an alliance, "nearer in its kind, and more durable, than any which is grounded upon treaties".(23) These expressions, to which many more might be added, are sufficient to prove that the opinions which produced the new colonial policy in the second quarter of the century were not confined to one particular sect, and that Southey had seen the vision of the British Empire as a Commonwealth of Nations as early as the year 1812. This, however, is a digression. Emigration was at best merely a possible ameliorative; it did not attempt to cure the diseases of English society by tackling them at their source.

It was only one of a formidable list of reforms demanded by Southey, a catalogue of which is given by his son. It includes national education, the diffusion of cheap and good literature, an organized system of colonization, with especial attention to the provision of female immigrants, a "wholesome training for the children of poverty", the establishment of Protestant sisters of charity and of a better class of hospital nurses, setting up of savings banks, abolition of flogging in the Services except in extreme cases, reform of the game laws, reduction in the number of capital crimes, execution of criminals within prison walls, reform of the factory system, establishment of national works in time of distress, allotments for labourers, employment of paupers in cultivating waste lands, commutation of tithes, an increase in the number of clergy, more colleges, and a more adequate judicial system. To these might be added various reforms for which he pleaded in the name of humanity, such as the abolition of bull-baiting and cock-fighting, improvements in prison conditions, more reputable ale-houses, and finally the cause of the little chimney-sweeps.(24) He gives a prominent place to law reform, allows that over-severe laws defeat their own ends; that the game laws are iniquitous, and that entail should be limited. But indeed, it would be a "Herculean task" "to clear away the rubbish of law, for in truth the pedantry and chicanery, and the insufferable delays, vexations and expense of law, are among the first evils of existing society".(25) Legal reform, all the same, was on its way; the new industrial system demanded a more efficient administration of the law. Some humanitarian reforms succeeded because they had behind them the force of the Evangelical revival. But the problem of poverty remained, in part to be solved by the unprecedented increase of national prosperity, in part to be handed down with all its attendant evils to subsequent generations.

Up to the present we have been describing the detailed reforms which the social theory of Coleridge and Southey stimulated them to propose; but what is most significant is their whole attitude towards economic facts. At the moment when a century of amazing industrial progress was commencing, theirs was the voice that uttered a warning that possibly something might be lost in the struggle for riches, that undesired results might manifest themselves, and that certain evils had already begun to appear. Coleridge and Southey in fact attribute most of the distress of contemporary England—rather unfairly—

to the operation of the commercial system and the accu-
mulation of large fortunes under it. "A people", writes
Southey, "may be too rich; because it is the tendency of
the commercial, and more especially of the manufacturing
system, to collect wealth rather than to diffuse it. Where
wealth is successfully employed in any of the speculations
of trade, its increase is in proportion to its amount:
great capitalists become like pikes in a fish-pond, who
devour the weaker fish; and it is but too certain that the
poverty of one part of the people seems to increase in the
same ratio as the riches of another."(26) During the
past generation, the number of wealthy individuals and
the national prosperity in a material sense had undoubtedly
increased, but, asks Coleridge, has the happiness of the
people increased proportionately? Have the people gained
anything from the manufacturing system but disease,
vice and pauperization? (27) Southey frankly denies that
the advantages of civilization have been at all adequately
shared by the poor, who, apart from the benefits of
religion, would be better off and happier as savages.(28)
Sentiments such as these indicate the basic connection
between the "back to nature" and the "back to the
Middle Ages" movements, and show how Southey the
revolutionist persisted in Southey the Tory. Rousseau,
Wordsworth, and the younger Southey represent the
former movement; the older Southey and Scott the
latter. For even in Scott is to be traced a similar distrust
of industrial civilization and suspicion that in proportion
as the *few* are raised, the many are "tantalized and
degraded".

In practice, of course, the social gap has been covered
over, though hardly bridged, by the existence of the
middle classes. Some realization of this fact led to the

formation of the theory held by Canning and other politicians of the importance of the middle classes as those "who cement the upper and lower orders of society, and who thereby blend together and harmonize the whole".(29) But the middle classes had not as yet achieved the position they were to occupy in the Victorian age, and the "two nations" were still in the most glaring contrast. Moreover, it was by no means certain on which side the "lower middle" would rank itself in the class war which seemed inevitable. About the year 1812, Crabb Robinson notes in his Diary, both Southey and Wordsworth were haunted with the fear of a social war between the rich and the poor. Scott writes to Southey at the same time, "You are quite right in apprehending a *Jacquerie*; the country is mined beneath our feet". Again in 1819, he believes that "upwards of 50,000 blackguards are ready to rise between Tyne and Wear".(30) Southey in works and letters monotonously reiterates the imminence of class-war, just as Coleridge denounces the revival of Jacobinism, and Wordsworth joins in the cry. What else, they asked, could be expected to result from the growth of a huge manufacturing population filled with a "dreadful sense of injustice, of intolerable misery, of intolerable wrongs, more formidable than any causes that have ever moved a people to insurrection". Here are "materials for explosion" ever under our feet. Only the army, writes Southey in 1812, stands between the country and a *bellum servile*. "What I dare not say publicly, is that there is yet danger from the army."(31)

IV

TRUE SOCIAL REFORM

Just as the Lake Poets were repelled by the individualistic school, so they were attracted by two thinkers
who allowed for and even exaggerated the claims of the
community. It was characteristic of Southey's honesty of
mind that he should declare his sympathy quite undeterred
by the fact that these two were the common butt of
politicians and the bogy of the Tories. To some extent
he realized himself why the doctrines of Spence and
Owen appealed to him. After a visit from the latter he
wrote that he was "neither more nor less than such a
Pantisocrat as I was in the days of my youth".(1) Such,
he might have added, as at heart he still was. He confessed that he could not but believe that to a community
of land society would come in the end; for the present
the idea should be left as a hope and a speculation,
though "these will not be mere matters of speculation
in the times which are rapidly coming on".(2) He admired
the Spencean Philanthropists in the first place because
they adopted a definite reasoned attitude and knew what
they wanted; they had a consciousness of ultimate purposes which rendered them in his eyes "infinitely more
respectable than the shallow orators who declaim about
Reform".(3) But the very fact of the partial truth in
their doctrines made them dangerous, while, as taught,
he says, going over in effect to the opposite camp, their
views are directly subversive of the peace and prosperity
of society.(4) Under present conditions community of
property would merely put a bonus on idleness. "Liberty

and Property are words which, in this free country, have hitherto gone together; and these persons must not attempt to subvert society for the sake of trying their theory upon the grand scale."(5)

It would appear, then, as though Southey's sympathy with Spence and Owen was purely intellectual in character. But that would not be like him. So long as existing society is not violently overthrown or dangerously undermined he is willing to welcome experiments and encourage innovation. Therefore he would allow the Spenceans to start an experimental community of their own. Again, Southey was very interested in the new co-operative associations, the effect of which, he inclined to believe, might ultimately be to revolutionize society peacefully.(6) As under this term there were included trades unions, productive gilds, and consumers' co-operative societies, he may take the credit of just prophecy. His mediaevalism was of service here in helping him to understand the new order of things. "I suspect", he wrote, "that in many things our forefathers were wiser than we are. Their gilds prevented trades from being over-stocked."(7) Another of Owen's plans which won his approval was the scheme for the employment of pauper labour on the land.(8) But although he calls Owen "that happiest and most beneficent and most practical of all enthusiasts", and echoes his indictment of the industrial system, Southey is far from being an Owenite, and when he criticizes Owen does indeed lay his finger on the weak spot in the latter's propaganda. "I differ *toto coelo* from Mr. Owen, of Lanark, in one main point. To build upon any other foundation than religion is building upon sand. But I admire his practical benevolence; I love his enthusiasm, and I go far with him in his earthly views."

222

The failure of Owen was justly to be ascribed in large measure to his unwillingness or inability to make allowances for religious prejudices, but Southey's criticism really goes deeper than that. He would say that it was precisely because of the inadequacy of their religious ideas that the projects of the social reformers were doomed to failure. The struggle with which society was rent seemed to him not so much between two classes of people as between two sets of ideas, two groups of forces, the economic and utilitarian warring against the ethical and religious. Coleridge follows up the point. "The constant gist of his discourse", writes Carlyle in his satiric description of the sage of Highgate, "was lamentation over the sunk condition of the world; which he recognized to be given up to Atheism and Materialism."(9) National civilization consists of both material and spiritual elements and Coleridge along with Southey and Wordsworth attributed the social evils of the day to the development of the former at the expense of the latter.

> The world is too much with us; late and soon,
> Getting and spending, we lay waste our hours.

While the spirit of material progress and the mechanic arts prevail, trade and manufactures may temporarily flourish, but the undue predominance of commercial interests in national life must in the end, he believed, be fatal to both culture and commerce.(10) While the development of science and industry proceeded without any corresponding improvement in religion or morals only ruin could follow. To the remedying of this unbalanced progress he and his friends looked for the only radical cure for social evils. He summarizes at the end of the *Lay Sermon* the change he wishes to see brought

223

about. "Our manufacturers must consent to regulations; our gentry must concern themselves in the education as well as in the instruction of their natural clients and dependents—must regard their estates as secured indeed from all human interference by every principle of law, and policy, but yet as offices of trust with duties to be performed, in the sight of God and their country. Let us become a better people, and the reform of all the public (real or supposed) grievances, which we use as pegs whereon to hang our own errors and defects, will follow of itself."(11)

The conclusion from these arguments is that he realized what so many reformers neglect—the importance of motive; the problem of social reform is for the Lake Poets fundamentally one of attitudes of mind, a psychological problem. The only really valuable reform is that won from the willing consent of free agents by an appeal to nobler views. The State, says Coleridge, going back on his factory children pamphlets, can do nothing but withhold artificial aids to an injurious system.(12) The devious paths into which attempts to generalize as to the rights and wrongs of State interference would lead were as yet hidden. Realizing the necessity of regulations, he can yet say that only those which manufacturers imposed on themselves voluntarily would be effective or morally valuable. All this emphasis on the voluntary motive and individual initiative of reform was very true on one side, but it showed that Coleridge had not realized the rightful claims of the social conscience against individuals acting in a way directly affecting society and offending against its principles. He forgot that moral development and institutional expression must progress side by side, that a measure of reform passed by Parliament is not, as

Idealist philosophers might have us believe, merely a passive registering of a new step taken by the social conscience; it is in itself a victory for some element in social life òver some other element, and it sets a precedent for future struggles.

Anyhow, it is a spiritual reformation that is wanted, and in this we may easily agree with Coleridge: the struggle of classes on the economic plane is only to be resolved on the moral plane. We can explain the idea in his mind better in the words of his disciple Maurice, than in his own. "The reorganizers of society", writes the prophet of Christian Socialism, "and the conservators of society are at variance because they start from the same vicious premises; because they tacitly assume land, goods, money, labour, some subjects of possession, to be the basis of society, and therefore wish to begin by changing or maintaining the conditions of that possession; whereas, the true radical reform and radical conservation must go deeper and say: 'Human relations not only should lie, but do lie beneath all these, and when you substitute—upon one pretext or another—property relations for these, you destroy our English life and English constitution, you introduce hopeless anarchy'." (13) Spiritual reform, enlightenment, is recognized by the Lake Poets, and as much in their Tory period as in their revolutionary youth, as the prime necessity; and this brings us to the last and most fundamental of their reforms—a national system of education.

Not least among the ideas Coleridge and Southey learnt from the Middle Ages was that government should be patriarchal or paternal in its attitude towards its subjects. Now the first duty of a paternal government seems to them to be to secure the moral welfare of its subjects,

P 225

for which reason a truly religious education is necessary. "Man, and man alone, is permitted to run wild. You plough your fields and harrow them; you have your scarifiers to make the ground clean; and if after all this weeds should spring up, the careful cultivator roots them out, by hand. But ignorance and misery and vice are allowed to grow, and blossom and seed, not on the waste alone, but in the very garden and pleasure ground of society and civilization." Such, says Southey, is in England called "preserving liberty".(14)

A third motive for universal education was provided by the religious enthusiasm of the Evangelical revival, and even by its "Bibliolatry", to use Coleridge's term. For, all the emphasis laid on the Bible being of little use if people could not read it, on strictly religious grounds the whole population had to be taught thus much: to this simple fact can be attributed in large measure the development of elementary education in England in the last century. Utilitarian propaganda was also pressing the cause of education. But whereas the utilitarian ideal of education was secular and anti-religious, the Evangelical agitation, for the time the more effective, intended, of course, an education definitely in the principles of the national religion. The lower classes, writes Southey, "must be instructed in accordance with the established religion; they must be fed with the milk of sound doctrine", and made "as ready to die for their Church and State as the Spaniards".(15) Coleridge in one place takes an equally limited view: the Bible, he says, provides in itself the best education the people can have, and all they need be taught is how to read it. In words reminiscent of Burke he goes on: "Of the labouring classes, who in all countries form the great majority of the inhabitants, more than this is not perhaps generally desirable—'They are not sought for in public counsel'."(16)

But this narrow view is not typical. In 1796, while still under the influence of Godwin and sharing his faith in the omnipotence of opinion and the ultimate triumph of reason, he had proclaimed his hope: "That All may know the TRUTH And that the TRUTH may make us FREE",(17) and the generous ideal of youth was never really abandoned. To those who thought that as social peace had been disturbed by the diffusion of a false light it might be restored by shutting off the people from all light, he returned an unhesitating denial. Inconveniences caused by the spread of a little education could be remedied only by making education universal. Moreover, as Southey puts it, "Ignorance is no preventive in these days. . . . All who have ears can hear sedition, and the more ignorant they are, the more easy is it to inflame them."(18) A bad government, says Coleridge, is destroyed by the people if they become enlightened; it inevitably falls with them if they are kept ignorant. But he does not base his claim for education on public expediency alone, though his timidity is a testimony to the strength of laissez-faire even in the enemy's camp. His inner thought, surviving from revolutionary days, is that education is a right and a duty, a benefit a man should receive simply because he is a man. How can educated men deny education to others? he asks in the *Friend*. In Southey the influence of youthful opinions is even more obvious. "As nature has given man all his faculties for use, any system of society in which the moral and intellectual powers of any portion of the people are left undeveloped for want of cultivation, or receive a perverse direction, is plainly opposed to the system of Nature, in other words, to the will of God."(19)

We have travelled nowadays far beyond the idea that because everyone should be able to read the Bible, therefore every child should be taught the alphabet. Nor was every good Christian so restricted in his educational outlook a hundred years ago. Reading and writing, says Coleridge, are a means in education, not its end: national education is something more than this. It means "educing the faculties and forming the habits" of civilized human beings.(20) Wordsworth's favourite topic, wrote Emerson after his visit to Rydal Mount, was the superficiality of the tuition that takes the place of education.(21) He, too, looked on education as a drawing-out process, including everything that contributes to physical, moral, and intellectual development. The Godwinian doctrine of the natural goodness of man is here brought into co-operation with a semi-Platonic theory of innate ideas. The development of the potentialities for good of the individual becomes the object of education, the imparting of knowledge no more than the means.

Of course, the Lake Poets' conception of the functions of education is not ours. They were still under the sway of the mediaeval conception of society as composed of hereditary classes, and of the Church as being by right the only institution through which men could enfranchise themselves, escape from their fixed social categories and become just individuals. In this respect, as all through, their thought is a curious mixture of the old and the new. The modern democrat may feel tempted to ridicule the feudal tone he rightly detects. Yet amend it slightly, and what have we but an anticipation of "My Station and its Duties"? It was well for England that even at the height of individualistic anarchy there were not wanting a few to bear witness to that truth and to hand on the torch. Southey was an early adviser of the Lord Shaftesbury of Factory Reform fame, and a correspondent of Owen. Coleridge exercised a critical influence over J. S. Mill, and gave the inspiration which moved the leaders of Christian Socialism. Certain obvious direct influences may be attributed to the Lake Poets, and their ideas, reiterated in pamphlet, book, magazine article, correspondence and conversation, cannot have been without influence on public opinion. More important for us than this, however, is their intrinsic value for the development of political and social theory. They bear witness to the discovery and deepening of that idea of the nation which Burke and Wordsworth had introduced. In the development of social ideal, Coleridge, Southey and Wordsworth form a group the importance of which may be estimated more highly when time has put nineteenth-century history into a truer perspective. Their conception of the community and its life may have seemed only a fragrant memory of mediaeval corporations and Greek city states, but it also held great promise for the future, for out of it sprang the social reforms advocated by the poets of romanticism and they testified in their turn to its concreteness and vitality.

NOTES

I 1. Corr. of Burke and Windham, 213.
2. Works, V. 89.
3. Acton has an interesting observation in this connection: "Burke's notion that small proprietors, not likely to increase, are the salt of the earth, begins the theory of middle-class government".

4. Samuels, op. cit., App. II, "The Reformer", No. 7.
5. Acton MSS. 4967.
6. Samuels, op. cit. 315.

II 1. Cobbett: Rural Rides (Everyman Edition), I. 179.
2. Essays, II. 237; Colloquies, I. 60; II. 276.
3. Colloquies, II. 221.
4. Wilberforce: Practical View of Christianity, 404–6.
5. Colloquies, I. 34.
6. Id. I. 110.
7. Church and State, 44–5.
8. Maitland: Collected Papers, I. 160–1.
9. Table Talk, 201.
10. Mill: Dissertations and Discussions, I. 452.
11. Table-Talk, 198–9; Letters, ed. Prideaux (1913), 18–19.
12. Friend, II. 139.
13. Letters, ed. Prideaux, 18–19.
14. Southey: Essays, I. 82.
15. Id. I. 154; II. 142–3, 259, 265–6.
16. Malthus: Essay on Population (ed. of 1803), MS. note by Coleridge, p. 11 (Br. Mus.).
17. Essays, I. 181.

III 1. Colls. I. 29; II. 425.
2. Lay Sermon, 426, 430, 435–6.
3. Lockhart: Life of Scott (1900), III. 130.
4. Malthus, op. cit. MS. note by Southey, p. 529.
5. Wordsworth: Prose Works (ed. Knight), II. 351.
6. Id. II. 350; Letters III. 450.
7. Essays, II. 211.
8. Colloquies, II. 253.
9. Id. I. 193.
10. Id. I. 182; Essays, I. 307.
11. Biographia Epistolaris, 141; Letters, 643.
12. Table-Talk, 282, 288.
13. Coleridge: Anima Poetae, 285; Lay Sermon, 439; Southey: Essays, I. 174; II, 225, 239.
14. Southey: Life and Corr. VI. 181.

15. Letters, ed. Prideaux, 18.
16. Colls. I. 167; Life and Corr. 200.
17. Letters, 689; May, 1818.
18. Crabb Robinson: Diary (1869), May 3, 1818; II. 93–4.
19. Two Addresses on Sir Robert Peel's Bill, ed. Gosse, 1913.
20. Essays, I. 72, II. 271, 274; Life and Corr. IV. 214, 357, V. 268, VI. 83, 181.
21. Sel. Lett. III. 374; Colloquies, II. 288.
22. Essays, I. 154.
23. Colloquies, II. 183.
24. Essays, I. 219, 224; II, 29, 117, 173, 176.
25. Colloquies, II. 208; Essays, I. 220, II. 177; Sel. Lett. III. 120.
26. Colloquies, I. 193.
27. Church and State, 67.
28. Letters from England, Espriella, I. 306–8; Colloquies, I. 46.
29. Canning: Speeches (1828), I. 149: 1799.
30. Lockhart, II. 218; III. 349.
31. Life and Corr. III. 335.

IV 1. Life and Corr. IV. 195.
2. Sel. Lett. III. 45; IV. 148.
3. Essays, I. 396.
4. Id. I. 411.
5. Id. I. 412.
6. Life and Corr. VI. 50; Sel. Lett. IV. 146–7.
7. Life and Corr. VI. 86.
8. Id. IV. 204; Essays, II. 24.
9. Carlyle: Life of Sterling (1905), II. 48.
10. Friend, III. 184–5.
11. Lay Sermon, 440.
12. Id. 433.
13. F. Maurice: Life of F. D. Maurice, II. 114.
14. Colloquies, I. 108.
15. Life and Corr. III. 343.
16. Statesman's Manual, 308–9

17. Prospectus of "The Watchman", 1796.
18. Life and Corr. IV. 28.
19. Colloquies, II. 411.
20. Statesman's Manual, 328; Essays on His Own Times, 702.
21. Emerson: English Traits (Everyman Edition), 9.

CHAPTER VIII

THE STATE AND RELIGION

I

THE RELIGIOUS REVIVAL

IT HAS ALREADY BEEN necessary for us on more than one occasion to mention the part religious ideas played in forming the political and social ideas of the Lake Poets and of Burke. In this chapter we propose to examine that influence in detail. How new a thing—for contemporaries —such influence was we can see if we call to mind the typical attitude on religious matters of the eighteenth century.

The spirit of that age was secular and rationalist, tolerant of the amiable weaknesses of religious men, but scarcely approving them, frightened above all of "enthusiasm". Outward conformity for the sake of setting a good example to the lower orders was combined with real spiritual indifference. So long as the recognized principles of morality and the traditional forms of worship were respected the eighteenth-century Church was satisfied. The inadequate nature of the orthodoxy of the day is conveyed with no great unfairness in Leslie Stephen's satiric version of Paley's creed. "Christ came to tell us that we should go to hell if our actions did not tend to promote the greatest happiness of the greatest number; and the Almighty has contrived a means for giving him satisfactory credentials. The man at whose order the clock strikes thirteen must be in the secret of the artificer,

233

and we may trust his account of a hidden part of the machinery." The sincerity of Paley and of many of the clergy is not in question, but their capacity for religious feeling was limited, and rationalism had sapped the foundations of the orthodox position.

From such generalizations the masses have to be excepted. We must remember, too, that while the older religious organizations seemed to be declining a new one was rapidly developing, in part to take their place, in part to meet the needs of a new industrial population. The comfortable post-prandial repose of official Anglicanism was rudely disturbed when Wesley and Whitfield swept like crusaders across the country. But while for the social historian Methodism is of prime importance, its function in the history of thought is almost negligible: it represented heat without light, is the rather cruel verdict of one critic. Moreover the party within the Church that was stimulated by Wesley into a like revivalist activity proved equally sterile, and Evangelicanism, like Methodism, found its merit and justification in the practical sphere. These movements represent a spontaneous response to a neglected emotional need rather than a change in the world of thought or any profound new development in human feeling. Their influence was widespread, however, and towards the end of the century even the higher ranks of society began to be affected by religious movements. The clear cold light of reason was waning and the trend in thought was away from the *raison* of the *philosophes*. Ethics also was falling back on the intuitive criterion and all round faith and feeling were taking the place of logic. Intellectualism had in effect abdicated and the stage was set for a full-blown religious revival.

234

This phenomenon has been explained as a reaction against the anti-clerical excesses of the Revolution, an explanation which mere chronology is sufficient to discountenance, since the revival had well begun long before the Revolution broke out. One must, however, confess inability to provide an alternative explanation. All we can truly say is that at this time occurred one of those mysterious changes in the mind of the people which, like the mental crises of individual experience, seem to come not in the logic of intellectual processes, but to well up fitfully from the unconscious. They arise like a sudden storm at sea: hardly a warning and we are in the midst of a hurricane that may tear all our ships from their anchorage and carry us utterly out of our bearings. An observer of the mid-eighteenth century might have felt safe enough in prophesying that, with the barque of European civilization well under the control of the *Aufklärung*, it would be a matter of only a few generations before it rode peacefully out of religious seas. The mutability of the human mind decreed otherwise.

It is not always realized how early the prophets of the religious revival began their work: Wesley opened his campaign in 1739; Rousseau published the *Lettre à d'Alembert*, which marked his breach with the *philosophes*, in 1758. Shortly afterwards he revised the already composed *Vicaire Savoyard*—a conversation between a young man and an old priest which is in effect a personal confession of faith—and included the new version in his *Émile*. In substance his system of belief comes to a deism not very different from that of Voltaire which we described in the first chapter, with the essential exception that by Rousseau it is amazingly re-charged with emotion. All eighteenth-century deism is a penny-plain version of

Christianity, but whereas Voltaire is still outward bound, Rousseau has rounded the cape of infidelity and is steering back to the faith of his fathers. "*Ce qu'il a cru être la religion de la nature*," writes P. M. Masson, "*ne fut que la religion de ses pères*."(1) With Rousseau the idea of Nature, which since the end of the Middle Ages had been increasingly turned against religion, is brought back into the fold. To the Libertines the appeal to nature had been a means of denying asceticism; to many writers of the eighteenth century—witness the early Rousseau himself—the natural had meant the uncivilized, the unartificial; for Nature the *philosophes* had read Reason. But to Rousseau Nature was another name for Providence. "*Ô Nâture, ô ma mère, me voici sous ta seule garde*." While he adopts the terms of the eighteenth century he infuses into them the ideas of the religious revival. It has been suggested that the religious movement was part of the democratic drift, in so far as it indicated an emergence of the religious ideas of the masses, and if so the place of Rousseau as reflecting the vague sentimentality of the people is clearly marked out. He took up a characteristically untenable intermediate position between orthodoxy and infidelity. Voltaire and his friends looked on him as a traitor, while the Church deemed his aid too dangerous to be welcome. Perhaps it was felt that in his religious invocations he was stealing the Christian thunder, but all the same there can be no doubt that for many years his influence powerfully stimulated the revival of Catholicism. The difficulty for Rousseau was that his deism was itself too bound up with the eighteenth century and its exaltation of the individual to prove a permanent altar of refuge to souls clutching at salvation. There were two ways of making a stand against the sceptical attack—by falling back on the conscience, a remedy too heroic for the majority, or by rallying round authority. And authority still waited, ever biding its time, bending before the usurper but knowing its latent power. As Renan explains, *"La catholicisme étant la plus characterisée . . . des religions toute réaction religieuse se fait nécessairement à sa profit".* So it was that Rousseau led on to Chateaubriand and the Theocrats. In the same way, as the Evangelical revival in England slowly lost its fire, its place was taken by Tractarianism.

The most important reason for the success of the Catholic revival and the comparative failure of other religious movements at the beginning of the nineteenth century is to be found in their relation to the general trend of contemporary thought. The eighteenth century and the revolutionary period, naturally favourable to individualism in religion as in every other sphere, had looked forward hopefully to the time when the increasing independence and separateness of the individual person should have brought a kind of Godwinian millennium into being. The generation that followed the Revolution, having learnt what happened when the individual enfranchised himself from social bonds, sought for some means of calling men back to their allegiance, of restoring the old uncritical obedience to rulers and linking up again the chains of custom. For such a restoration of society religion seemed the only stable basis and among religions especially the Catholic Church. So argued the Theocrats, following out the idea Burke had thrown out at the very beginning of the Revolution. But along the strictly religious line possibility of advance was limited by the capacity of Rome to develop. The process that began with Rousseau and Chateaubriand and Lamennais ended with Antonelli and the Syllabus of 1864, when the liberalism of Pio Nono gave way before the pressure of circumstance and of tradition. In explanation of the weakness inherent in the Catholic revival it may be suggested, first, that although not caused, it was certainly assisted by the reaction against the Revolution, and so naturally decayed as the Revolution came to be forgotten; and secondly, that the whole religious revival was itself only a symptom, that it prospered for a time because it found itself in sympathy with the spirit of a new age, and then ceased to advance because, tied to the rigid ideas and vested interests of old organizations, it found itself in ultimate conflict with that same spirit.

II

THE DEFENCE OF THE ANGLICAN CHURCH

What now, we must ask, was the share of Burke, and the others associated with him in this study, in the religious revival? It is easily seen that they were all profoundly religious, Burke himself manifesting from beginning to end a religious spirit and devout temper rare in an eighteenth-century politician. When he visited France in 1773, the brilliant society of the Paris *salons* courted the great English leader of opposition. Mme du Deffand told Horace Walpole, "He will leave pleased with our nation". He left, as we know, disgusted at their fashionable scepticism, and in the same year writes that the cruellest blow against civil society is atheism. The object of one of his first works had been to defend religion by showing that society and religion stand and fall together. Bolingbroke having attacked revealed religion as an artificial addition to natural religion, Burke tries to show that in the same way political society can be condemned as an artificial addition to natural society. It was characteristic of himself and of his age that he did not attempt to go to the root of the fallacy and deny altogether the validity of the distinction between artificial and natural. He was content to accept the common ideas of his time, joining on to them the new ideas that his insight gave him, but seldom or never challenging the old.

In his conception of the divine fabric of the universe and the Providential ordering of human life, although clothing the idea with an eloquence and infusing into it an emotional conviction paralleled in that century only by Rousseau, Burke introduced nothing specifically new. The direct application of his principles in politics did not come till the Revolution had aroused him to a keener sense of the dangers resulting from irreligion. Then it was that he felt called upon to impress again and again, on the listening mind of Europe rather than on the drowsy intellects of his fellow-legislators, the lesson that the permanence of the political order was dependent on the stability of its religious foundations. Religion is "the grand prejudice, and that which holds all other prejudice together". Man, he asserts in the *Reflections*, is a religious animal, who, were Christianity abandoned, would relapse into degrading superstitions, choosing a false religion rather than none at all.

We must remember in considering his religious theories that too often Burke's dialectical power and profound insight are put merely to the task of defending the *status quo*, and this is the case with his views on the relation of religion and politics. It cannot be denied that the political

benefits conferred by religious organizations, in particular
by the Church of England, tend in his mind, as in the
minds of most of his contemporaries, to outweigh spiritual
values. He cannot be accused of localizing religion to
the degree attained by Fielding's parson: "When I say
religion, I mean the Christian religion; and when I say
the Christian religion, I mean the Protestant religion; and
when I say the Protestant religion, I mean the Church of
England." Still, Burke is an uncompromising supporter
of the principle of a National Church, and while requiring
that the State shall protect the Church and recognize its
claim to a share in the ordering of the life of the community, he gives it in return an extensive right of control
over the Church. He made his position clear in the debate
in 1772 on the clerical petition for relief from subscrip-
tion to the Articles. What the State required of the clergy,
according to him, was "not a conformity of private but
of public opinion"; this for the sake of peace and decorum.
He refused to discuss "how much truth is preferable to
peace", because the latter is so much more certain that
it could scarcely ever be justifiable to imperil it for the
sake of the phantasmal benefits of speculative truth. In
the *Annual Register* is a summary by himself of the
arguments he used on this occasion. He showed "that a
supreme controlling power was inherent in every legislature", "that all governments had a right to constitute the
several orders of their subjects as they pleased", and
"that it was necessary that those who were appointed to
be the public teachers and instructors of the people,
should be bound by some certain principles from which
they were not to deviate".(1) "We must have", his
collected speeches say, "some criterion of faith more brief,
more precise and definite than the Scripture for the
240

regulation of the priesthood." "I would have a system of religious laws that would remain fixed and permanent, like our civil constitution." Lacking this, men could save themselves from constant religious change only by submitting to the authority of a spiritual dictator, such, he implies, as the Pope(2)—precisely the argument, it is interesting to note, which, employed later in quite a different context, led him to the famous prophesy of Napoleon. It was on the same grounds that the Greeks had believed that a State must either recognize *nomos*—customary law —or else pass into a tyranny.

Burke accepts the national church as it stands and devotes himself to the provision of arguments in defence of the system without any comprehensive attempt at analysing it. The ecclesiastical problem was, on the other hand, a branch of political theory to which Coleridge devoted much anxious thought, and on which he wrote his only systematic treatise. In the *Church and State* he begins by making clear the terminology he proposes to use. To the word "church" he gives a triple significance. In the largest sense it includes the universal Christian Church; in a narrower sense, only a particular national religious organization. The former, too, the Church of Christ outward and visible, must not be confounded with a third community, the spiritual and invisible Church, known only to God: a confusion which, he says, has to account for much intolerance and error in the past. That is to say, essentially religion is a matter for individuals. The body of true believers form a mystical community apart from and not identical with the Church visible and militant. But even in this second sense the Church belongs to a realm of its own, and can have no relation with the States of this world, from which it asks nothing but protection from interference and to be let alone.(3) It must not be confused with the National Church, which is the organization presiding over religious worship in the State. It is of the Church in this third sense that the clergy are officers; for the Church of Christ—both as the visible and as the mystical Church—has none.(4) Thus Bishops hold their position in Convocation as Prelates of the National Church and their seats in the House of Lords as Peers, and their powers in these offices are temporal. It follows from all this that to Coleridge the eighteenth-century conception of Christianity as part of the law of England is absurd: instead, Christianity is, in relation to the National Church, merely a "blessed accident".(5)

Turning to the National Church, he observes that this is the constitutional organ for the attainment of certain of the ends of the State. The first is to secure for all its members the hope of bettering their condition and that of their children. The duty of the Church is to draw all the most deserving from the lower classes and elevate them to their rightful rank in society. Coleridge is plainly thinking of the mediaeval rather than of the modern Church when he says its function is to mediate between the rich and the poor, between the Government and the people. Instead of this, at the Reformation, he holds, the English Church had committed the fatal error of clinging to king and court in preference to grounding its hopes on the grateful affections of the people. By breaking away from the Roman Church it ceased to be extra national, but only to become royal.(6) Thus the Established Church can never be said to have filled adequately this first purpose of its establishment. The other ends which it should serve in the State, according to Coleridge, are to develop those faculties of the individual which qualify him to be a free citizen, and to safeguard national civilization.(7) The latter it achieves especially by providing for the existence of a class of persons with sufficient leisure and inclination to cultivate the higher things in life. A certain proportion of speculative minds he believes to be necessary to any civilized State; it is for the support of these that the Church has been endowed with property by the nation, which property Coleridge hence terms the "Nationalty". It belongs to the clergy as functionaries of the National Church only, and they are not the only rightful recipients. To use Coleridge's term, the whole "clerisy" of the land has the right of sharing the Nationalty, as it did in effect during the Middle Ages. Gradually the professions separated from the clergy proper, but this fact does not in any way affect the rights of those left behind; though the only wrongful use to which the Nationalty can be put is if it is alienated from its original purpose, as was so much Church land at the time of Henry VIII's Reformation. The purposes to which Church property can rightly be put Coleridge divides under four heads: (i) the maintenance of Universities and great schools, (ii) the maintenance of a pastor and schoolmaster in every parish, (iii) the building and repair of church and school buildings, (iv) the support of the aged and infirm. These involved the existence of a learned order, of which the smaller number were concentrated at the Universities, the remainder being scattered throughout the country. The parish priest and schoolmaster could in this way be regarded as transplanting a germ of civilization to every corner of the land.(8) Coleridge thus vindicated once and for all, against the attacks of Bentham and Adam Smith, the principle of an endowed class for the cultivation and spread of learning: so says John Stuart Mill, who learnt that lesson from him.(9)

To us these ideas may seem ordinary though idealistic, but they were novel and badly needed in Coleridge's day. The most significant feature in his discussion of the whole problem is the greatly expanded interpretation he puts on the word "church". It is no exaggeration to say that for him religion, far from being a mere collection of dogmas, comes very near being the sum-total of all that is true and good and beautiful in life. For any approximation in actual facts to Coleridge's idea we should have to go back to the best days of Greece. The truth is he was dreaming of such a religion as never was on sea or land. His position re-orientates the whole problem of Church and State, lifts the controversy on to a higher plane than that of partisan and sectarian feud, and enables him to combine what was noblest in many different answers to the problem in a way that passed the comprehension of his fellows.

III

SIGNIFICANCE OF THE RELIGIOUS REVIVAL

It is with Coleridge's idea of the Church in our minds that we must read such statements as those of Burke and Southey on the identification of Church and State in England. They are, says Southey, quoting Burke, "one and the same thing, being different integral parts of the same whole".(1) This must not be interpreted as merely implying the eighteenth-century "alliance": it goes far beyond the Tory-Anglican theory of alliance, which

according to Burke is but "an idle and fanciful speculation". Rather the English Church and State are in his
opinion identical, and the religious organization is not a
mere representation of individuals but "an oblation of
the State itself, as a worthy offering on the high altar of
universal praise". Language of this kind carries us into
an intellectual atmosphere very different from that of the
eighteenth century, and in order to understand the
attitude of Burke and Coleridge to the Church we must
pursue our inquiries further into the nature of the religious
revival.

The clue is to be found not so much in the strictly
religious as in the philosophical history of the eighteenth
century. It has been shown in the first chapter that
Lockian philosophy reached what was for many a *reductio
ad absurdum* in the teachings of Hume. Moreover, Hume
was not a solitary genius; he was but the earliest and most
able representative of the wave of scepticism which, says
Leslie Stephen, seems to sweep over the mind of Europe
in the middle of the century. The men of the earlier half
of the century had been comfortable optimists, satisfied
that they knew most of what man can know and content to
have reached as near perfection in their social and political
arrangements as men were likely to. The period between
the Seven Years War and the Revolution sees the emergence of a more pessimistic and sceptical spirit, a reaction
among the thinking few against the facile and futile
optimism which is the first result of a smattering of the
ideas of the *philosophes*.

The work of Hume was largely negative. All the same,
no constructive work was likely to be done in the world
of philosophy except by those who had realized the power
of the sceptical attack. The first thinker to attempt to

meet the difficulties propounded by Hume was Kant,
who saw that the great obstacle to philosophic advance
was the radical opposition of subjective and objective
reality, in the cleavage between which all secure knowledge
of the universe fell to the ground. The problem, he saw,
was—how to obtain knowledge about objective reality
which should have the same certainty as our knowledge
of subjective truth; or, in his own language, how are
synthetic propositions possible *a priori*?(2) This problem
Kant solves by what he calls critical or transcendental
idealism, meaning by this the reference of our cognitions
not to things in themselves but to the faculty by which
they are cognized. In a sense this avoids the question, for
the effort to know things in themselves is frankly abandoned. The perceptions resulting from the impact of
these supposed things in themselves on the human mind
are taken as the ultimate material with which philosophy
has to deal, behind which from the very nature of knowledge it cannot go. They are valid subjectively, it is argued,
because we are aware that they form a definite part of a
particular state of our consciousness. Universal validity
results when each perception is brought into connection
with the whole world of consciousness. This is accom-
plished by referring each individual perception to some
general concept, or, as Kant would say, *a priori* intuition.
Thus every white object, to take a simple example, is
referred to the abstract idea of whiteness. The sum of all
individual perceptions, thus understood through concepts,
is the philosopher's Nature, the reality of which is consequently *a priori*. The reality of Nature is thus the same
as the reality of the mind; truth for the one is the same
as truth for the other, and the mind is itself a creative
force in the shaping of that truth, no longer merely a

passive agent. The human mind is thus emancipated from the bonds of the sensational psychology and the tyranny of the empirical is overthrown.

Coleridge has said that the psychology of the State is but a magnified version of the psychology of the individual and that it is in this light that Plato's *Republic* must be read. We may expand the application of this theory and say that similarly the revolt against Locke's psychology was not without influence in the changing attitude to the State that developed at the same time. This latter was most marked in those thinkers who shared explicitly or implicitly in the former movement. Running these through our mind—such thinkers as Rousseau and Burke, Wordsworth, Coleridge, Kant, Hegel and others—we cannot help seeing that at any rate in its more philosophic manifestations the change has obvious affiliations with the religious revival. Many other names could be added, their divergencies being sufficient to prove that the movement was not essentially connected with any particular form of religious orthodoxy. In general we can say it was marked by a mystical tendency which drew its inspiration from many and different quarters. This emphasis on the spiritual relations between the individual soul and God, this consciousness of a unity running through all things, in a word, of divine immanence, appears in German Pietism, in the doctrines of the Moravians, in the fantastic religiosity of the *illuminés*, in more orthodox form as Schliemacher's rehabilitation of Christianity, and under a philosophic cloak in the works of Schelling and Hegel. In England the Non-Jurors had kept alive a mystical tradition, and though the philosophical movement originated by Kant was for long confined to Germany, England showed certain tendencies in the same direction. Some of the neo-Platonists were translated about the end of the century by T. Taylor, and Coleridge, who as we know from a famous essay of Lamb, was early acquainted with Iamblichus and Plotinus, rapidly abandoned Godwin's arid creed for a more stimulating philosophy. He was confirmed in his courses by the influence of Spinoza and later on came to know the writings of some of the German Idealists. In the attempt to reconcile German Idealism with Pauline Christianity he spent unavailingly his greatest powers.

The religious, philosophical and psychological theories of Coleridge, and to a lesser extent of Wordsworth, are of importance for us because in these two thinkers their connection with the new outlook on politics is most plainly marked. Further, we cannot help seeing that Coleridge and Wordsworth are expressing in a religious form the same ideas that in Kant and Hegel take philosophic shape. The parallel between Wordsworth and Hegel has been pointed out by other writers.(3) For them both Mind is the universal principle in nature and man, and mind is not the simple analytic reason of the *philosophes*, it is a spiritual force which the individual can apprehend only by virtue of direct intuition. There is at least one important corollary which they draw from this: that the relationship of individuals with each other is not a mere external contact between entities for ever separate, but is a meeting and interpenetration of mutually affected individual minds in a universe of mind. Apply this to the community at large, and what room is left for the artificial aggregate of the eighteenth century? We have in its place a community bound together by ties stronger though more impalpable than any dreamed of by the Lockian school. Moreover, its unity is in the nature of things a unity of the mind; it is a spiritual community. Two rival interpretations of it appeared—the metaphysical State of Hegel and the national community of Burke and the Lake Poets. Surely it is not too much to believe that the latter has stood the test of time rather better than the State of the Idealists? The point with which we are concerned at this moment, however, is to establish the influence of the religious and philosophical changes of the end of the eighteenth century over political thinking. The practical conclusion of that influence was the reclaiming of the secular State for the spiritual sphere, and in this sense must we understand what Coleridge, for instance, says of the national religion. The State, considered in this light, is no simple utilitarian convenience. it is a spiritual community cohering by virtue of an inner necessity. Not in a narrow sectarian sense, but in a broader way of speaking, the State itself is a religious community, and if the existence of a national Church can be justified it can only be as an expression of that fundamental truth.

NOTES

I 1. P. M. Masson: La Religion de Rousseau (1916), II. 293.

II 1. Annual Register, 1772, 88–9.
   2. Speeches, I. 100: 1772.
   3. Church and State, 126, 127, 139.
   4. MS. note to "A Charge," by C. J. Bloomfield, 1830, pp. 10–11 (Br. Mus.).
   5. Church and State, 59.
   6. Table-Talk, 106, 187.
   7. Church and State, 47, 76.

8. Church and State, passim; Literary Remains, IV.
   151, III. 119; Biog. Lit. 110–111.
9. Mill: Dissertations and Discussions, I. 445.

III 1. Essays, II. 368.
    2. Prolegomena to any Future Metaphysic, ed. Mahaffy
       and Bernard, 1915.
    3. A. C. Bradley: English Poetry and German Philosophy
       (1909).

CHAPTER IX

THE REVOLT AGAINST THE EIGHTEENTH CENTURY

I

THE REVOLT AGAINST THE SENSATIONAL PSY-CHOLOGY: SENTIMENTALISM AND BACK TO NATURE

THE RELIGIOUS REVIVAL was evidently not the decisive fact in the revolt against the eighteenth century. As one by one the different religious movements lost their initial ardour, it was seen that they belonged to a constantly recurring and essentially evanescent type of phenomena. They revived old religious institutions and created new ones, but they introduced nothing into Western civilization that was not already in existence, and they presented no permanent obstacle to the advance of eighteenth-century ideas. The eighteenth century, insurgent in the Revolution, did but stay its course for a brief space; its principles swept over into the next century with accumulated force, on the crest of a wave mounting higher and higher as it rushed on, as it rushes on to-day— towards we know not yet what goal.

But though there was nothing that could answer eighteenth-century criticism satisfactorily in the Wesleyan and Evangelical movements, in the Catholic revival and in Tractarianism, this is not to say that there were not religious thinkers whose views, if given a hearing, were capable of modifying profoundly and perhaps even entirely upsetting the eighteenth-century world-view. The Revolution, we must agree, was but the culmination of the previous century. But among the eddying and swirling waters of the revolutionary period are signs of another and very different current, come thither from unknown seas, surging upward from unfathomed depths. Almost contemporaneously, in England, France and Germany, appear three thinkers—Burke, Rousseau and Kant—whose influence, acting through various forms, was to undermine much that the eighteenth century had believed in profoundly. The influence of Burke was primarily political, that of Kant philosophic and that of Rousseau literary and religious.

An ill-assorted company they seem, the Anglo-Irish party orator, the old philosopher of Königsberg, and the wild, fleeting, inspired Genevese. What could they have in common—save that each was in revolt against the eighteenth century? Now to be in revolt against that century was essentially to be in revolt against a theory of the mind—that superficial psychology of sensations described above. It is in their revolt against the psychological school founded by Locke that Burke, Rousseau and Kant find a principle of union, and it would not be untrue to say that they were all three inspired less by the scientific weakness of this theory than by its inability to satisfy the eternal demand of the human spirit for a sense of reality. For Lockian psychology seemed to admit the reality only of things of immediate perception. Hence for Burke it excluded from politics the whole field of tradition, the whole work of the genius of the race; for Rousseau it prohibited that penumbra of the conscious mind on which he relied to supply him with artistic and religious inspiration; and, for Kant, by making the scepticism of Hume unavoidable, it denied the possibility of philosophic truth.

Like the religious revival, however, the break away from Lockian psychology proved inadequate in itself to overthrow the ideas of the *philosophes*. If it had not been so the eighteenth-century system would have collapsed before it had well begun, because the sensational psychology showed signs of developing inconsistently from the very beginning. Let us trace this process. As befitted an intensely didactic age, one of the principal problems of Locke's school was the problem of ethics. The old religious sanctions had vanished and were to be replaced by utilitarianism, as we saw in the first chapter. Utilitarianism, moreover, was interpreted in a very narrow rationalistic sense, and being combined with a strict individualism it presented the problem of the reconciliation of the interests of the individual with those of the rest of the community in an acute form. A section of opinion represented by Mandeville's *Fable of the Bees* solved the problem by apotheosizing selfishness and calling it universal harmony; the philosophical radicals and some of the economists accepted this solution. Another, and for a time a more influential school of thought, in effect abandoned the severe individualism of the stricter utilitarians. They incorporated social virtue into the conception of man's nature in the form of a "moral sense". Universal harmony, says Shaftesbury, the leader of this school, is represented in man by an innate principle of morality. To accept this was to admit a considerable breach in the fabric of Locke's system; it was fatal to strict rationalism.

The reaction is carried a stage further by Hume, who adopts Shaftesbury's moral sense as an alternative to Locke's deductive ethics. For Hume, however, this is only part of a general campaign against intellectualist theories of the mind. By the mechanism of association he is able to explain the working of the mind without the intervention of a rational faculty. He holds that "when the mind passes from the idea or impression of one object to the idea or belief of another, it is not determined by reason, but by certain principles, which associate together the ideas of these objects, and unite them in the imagination".(1) By means of this theory he is enabled to purge thought and knowledge of their rational element and to reduce opinion and belief to simple feeling, "more properly an act of the sensitive, than of the cogitative part of our natures".(2) Nor does it derogate from their significance and validity for him that moral and political opinions are only sentiments. Rejecting intellectualism and the deductive ethics of Locke, he does not fall back on the moral scepticism of Hobbes. Inexorable custom and the unfailing passions of man provide him with a point of rest less elusive than the arguments of the abstract reason. For the reason is a vain thing, he says, which by its very nature is incapable of motivating the will; only the passions can do that.(3) Hence, as moral philosophy is a practical science aiming at practical results, it cannot be derived from the reason.(4) Thus, declining to derive morality from either supernatural ordinance or from a rationalistic calculation of consequences, he is left with the necessity of deriving it from sentiment or feeling.(5)

This same tendency, which in Hume took philosophic shape, was represented for his contemporaries by a literary phenomenon. We need not look further than to the arid utilitarianism and the gross materialism which formed the popular interpretation of the ideas of the school of Locke for an explanation of the wave of sentimentality in the latter half of the century. The sentimentalists are of little importance in the history of thought, nevertheless this phase marks the first line of revolt against intellectualism and the beginning of the reassertion of the actual individual. Moreover, the greatest of the sentimentalists—such as Diderot and Rousseau in France—represent something more than mere sentiment. They mark a further stage in the movement back to reality. Sentiment is the first step, an effort towards simplification the second; and both of these are absorbed in the broader movement, that "return to nature" with which romanticism is inaugurated.

With Rousseau, the petty bourgeois, started the cult of the wild, unregulated, primitive passions, of barbaric nature and of innocent, uncivilized natural man. Nothing that Rousseau wrote subsequently ever effaced the memory of his first essay. This was only fair, for the note which he struck in the *Discours sur les Arts et les Sciences* is heard again and again, in the *Émile*, the *Nouvelle Héloïse*, and at the end of his life in the *Méditations d'un promeneur solitaire*. Nature, in all the various meanings of that much-abused word, was the goddess of Rousseau's adoration. Naturalism, of course, had been the result for the whole Enlightenment of the abandonment of the religious attitude; but the austere Nature deity of Voltaire appeared transformed by Dionysiac traits at the hands of the author of the *Confessions*. The importance of this transformation must not be exaggerated, however: it was not this side of Rousseau's teachings which counted politically. The influence of the sentimentalists is to be found rather in literature, in religion, and in social movements—in the floods of sentiment that deluged the revolutionary assemblies and that poured from the printing presses of France, Germany and England, in the religious history of a Chateaubriand, in the increasing simplicity of dress, and in the lachrymose sensuality that saw a child of nature in every errant Marquise.

Still, Rousseau did have at times a true if theatrical vision of nature, and could see a mountain or a forest as it had not been seen before; and after him, along the same path came greater and sincerer men, for whom, moreover, nature had a new meaning. For Wordsworth nature was not merely the uncivilized, the primitive, the world as yet untouched by man, but man himself was part of nature. Wordsworth and his contemporaries loved Nature as perhaps no generation before or since, for they saw in her not only infinite beauty, but behind the ceaseless mutations of changing colour and transient scene they knew her at heart, the mysterious mother of humanity, brooding in omnipresence. The Renaissance had discovered Man; it was left for Romanticism to make the real discovery of Nature, and wondering to guess "with a wild surmise" at who knows what arcana hidden therein from unpoetic gaze. In Wordsworth, more than in any other poet of nature, was the feeling greater than simple appreciation of natural beauty; it was more even than a consciousness of secret sympathies between nature and man; it was a knowledge of oneness with all the animate and inanimate world, a refusal to put nature on one side and man on the other and leave them thus eternally divided; it was a faith reaching in many a glowing invocation almost to pantheism.

> Dust as we are, the immortal spirit grows
> Like harmony in music; there is a dark
> Inscrutable workmanship that reconciles
> Discordant elements, makes them cling together
> In one society.(6)

From a literary point of view we are now in the midst of the revolt against the eighteenth century, but as regards politics it is altogether a different matter. "Nature" is a term which may mean much or little—or sometimes nothing at all. Politically, "back to nature" was captured by the Revolution; thus illustrating the manner in which the fundamental tendencies of an age persist through apparent changes in terminology and remould themselves to suit a new spirit. The Nature of most of the romanticists is simply an emotionalized version of the Reason of the *philosophes*, its political effect being to place their views of society in a democratic setting. Thus it was that the leaders of the second generation of romanticism in England—to give only two names, Shelley and Byron—were descendants of the eighteenth-century system of thought, inspired by a sentimentalized version of the ideas of the *philosophes*, rather than by those of Wordsworth, Coleridge and Burke. The sentimental and naturalistic movements, beginning in a revolt against the intellectualist theory of the mind, ended by declining into a mere superficial ornamentation to a view of man and society, and their place in nature, which was in fact based on that intellectualist psychology itself. This revolt against the eighteenth century had thus failed, and failed badly, and that precisely because it took the first and easiest line of attack. The Ideas of the Enlightenment were of no great philosophic profundity, but they were not to be overcome in favour of such a baseless fabric as the romanticism of the sentimental and "back to nature" school.

Herein lay the essential weakness of Rousseau, and the explanation of the ineffectiveness of his ideas in the realm of practical politics. Burke himself had never had any truck with these tendencies, but the youthful fancy of the Lake Poets had been captivated at once. Yet though sentimentalism and naturalism left a lasting mark on their contribution to English literature, the influence on their ideas in general was very transitory and passed away with the waning of their revolutionary enthusiasm. If we are to find a clue to their political or social philosophy it is certainly not to be found in this.

II

THE INFLUENCE OF THE HISTORIC IDEA

The religious revival, sentimentalism, and "back to nature", though they all have some connections with the political thought of Burke and the Lake Poets, obviously fail to provide us with a satisfactory clue to the inmost nature of their revolt against the prevailing system of ideas. It we turn back to our chapters on Burke, we will remember that very closely connected with his religious views was his idea of the nation as a community held together by long tradition, in other words by history. The belief that political values are to be judged in their relation with the historical community seemed to us the final teaching of Burke's political theory, and the lesson which the Lake Poets learned from him. Perhaps in this historic idea is to be found the ultimate explanation of what was original in the theory of Burke's followers as well as in his own theory: perhaps a historical sense is the creative force in their revolt against the eighteenth century. As Renan writes, "*L'histoire est la vraie philosophie du XIXe siècle*": it certainly was not of the eighteenth.

258

On the whole it is true to say that the sense of historical background, implicit in the philosophy which the Middle Ages had derived from the *Civitas Dei*, had been obscured since the decline of mediaeval theology. There lingered, however, even in the ideology occasioned by a Protestant environment, a belief in Providence and in the value of the traditional and customary. The eighteenth century changed all this. Confident in the power of reason, it challenged all existing creeds and institutions with the test of reasonableness and utility, ignoring completely the play of historic forces which had gone to their shaping, and looking for nothing but conscious and self-interested motives from the actors in the great drama of history.

It is true that quite early in the century there appeared a thinker for whom the history of man was more than a mere set of chronologically related but fortuitous phenomena. Vico definitely describes his *Scienza Nuova* as a "history of the ideas, customs and actions of the human race".(1) But Vico, whether because Italy was out of the main stream of European thought, or because his views were too novel and too far in advance of his time, failed to gain a hearing. Montesquieu incorporated some of his principles in the *Esprit des Lois*, but the glimpses of historical method in this work are far more rudimentary. The French writer lays great stress on the universal rule of law, an idea he derives from Vico, and he recognizes also the need to allow for the influence of physical environment in studying the varying customs of different peoples, but that is as far as he goes. The relativity of institutions in time does not enter his mind; no attempt is made to conceive history as more than a useful storehouse of precedents. Bolingbroke, despite his pompous "philosophy teaching by examples' phrase," is equally unenlightened.

Similarly, Hume, although he turned to historical writing in his later years, revealed only a chronicler's conception of events. Leslie Stephen has attributed the defects of Hume and of most contemporary historians to their narrow view of their own functions as discoverers of causal relations among the phenomena they had to describe. Now as Hume's philosophy contained a destructive criticism of the very idea of causation, this was only to be expected in His case. His *Essays*, on the other hand, show some disposition to generalize from historical evidence. There was great progress in the writing of history at this time, but it was principally in technique, in the searching out and more critical examination of evidence. History remained an external account with the usual intellectualist bias.

In the midst of so much historical research, men were bound to begin to look for something more from their material. But this they were not likely to get so long as they remained subject to the intellectualist psychology and extreme individualism of the school of Locke. History was bound to be a curiously distorted study so long as its characters were assumed to act always rationally and on motives of self-interest. It was bound to be an aimless phantasmagoria unless some relation besides that of a chronological succession of events was found in it, which meant unless it dealt with some entities more permanent than fleeting unrelated individuals. The intellectualist psychology had been undermined early, and so the more serious problem for historians was to find some corrective or supplement for the individualist theory of society. The first attempted solution was Voltaire's "history of civilization", a *genre* of historiography in which the subject became not men but Man.

Two favourite principles of the eighteenth century—empiricism and universality—were united in the idea of humanity which perhaps formed Voltaire's greatest contribution to the development of modern thought. His idea is to be distinguished from mere cosmopolitanism; it was the rebirth of the ecumenical idea, forgotten since the decline of Stoicism in the ancient world and the shattering of the Roman Empire—for the mediaeval outlook was parochial, if at the same time eternal. Mediaeval man was a citizen of the City of God and a member of the Church of Christ on earth; he was a subject of a local lord, but he was not a citizen of the world. Voltaire's philosophy as well as his pose made him essentially such, and under his teaching the Enlightenment learned to despise local and national prejudices. His success was only negative, for he found few followers to develop the positive aspects of his idea, and the religion of humanity as the revolutionaries tried to develop it proved a sorry farce. Individualism captured the idea of humanity and turned it into an invertebrate cosmopolitanism, which soon collapsed under the stress of the national and racial jealousies of the following century.

The next attempt to give substance to the historic idea came not from a professed historian but from the English statesman, Burke, and he, unconscious that he was sharing in an epoch-making discovery, ignorant of the world-shattering events that were to follow when the people of Europe came for themselves to the same realization, applied it to the national community, and so doing gained for himself a place among the prime founders of nationalism.

When, however, we speak of the thought of Burke and his successors as historical, it can only be with certain qualifications. Their merit was to have introduced general conceptions into the view of history. But it was not without reason that Wordsworth was described by his biographer as a thinker with "small value for anything but contemporary history".(2) Although this statement is not strictly true, certainly his historical feeling was manifested in a very different way from that of Savigny and his generation. To Burke, Wordsworth and Southey, history was primarily a religious process; to Coleridge, as a disciple of the Idealists, it was partly also a philosophic unrolling of ideas; and both the providential views of Burke's followers and the dialectical evolution of the Idealists were in rivalry rather than in alliance with the true historical movement. Yet, as Leslie Stephen has pointed out, history found its disciples in the ranks of the intuitionists, while the empirical school, which professed to base itself on experience, totally neglected historical evidence. It was not until the empiricism of the one school and the evolutionary ideas of the other had become linked that the historical movement proper was possible. Meanwhile, the conservatism of Burke and the early Romantic poets could be described as religious or philosophic rather than historical. Though there is a certain relationship, no logically inevitable connection exists between the historical movement proper of the nineteenth century and that historic conception of society which played so large a part in early Romantic political theory in England, and which was perhaps even the nucleus of romanticism.

Let us leave for a moment the broad principles and consider in more detail to what in fact the historical spirit of the Lake Poets amounted. Southey alone was a professed historian, and apart from the biographies of Nelson and
262

Wesley the work that won him his reputation is almost completely forgotten. Those huge tomes on South American history rest undisturbed on their shelves; Anglicanism does not now go for support to the *Book of the Church*. But Southey's labours must not be dismissed as altogether fruitless. He helped to elevate both the standard and the reputation of his own class of writers. Contemporaries were more appreciative of his historical talents than posterity has proved, and he himself perhaps gained more than any from his studies. They moderated a mind naturally prone to take extreme views and deepened a naturally superficial understanding. "A man", he wrote, "ought well to have studied history before he is fit for any direct share in national policy", (3) and such signs of political and social enlightenment above the ordinary as we discover in him are to be attributed in large measure to his own historical studies.

The revival of history had involved the discovery of the Middle Ages, of which Southey had been a close student. The main effect on him, as on his generation, was to substitute an idealized mediaevalism for the equally idealized and even more misconceived classicism of the eighteenth century. How the Romantic movement discovered the Middle Ages, and how the Middle Ages reacted on the romanticists by revealing to them a set of ideas which, wholly alien from the ideas of the eighteenth century and almost forgotten, were yet the original basis of the customs and institutions of pre-revolutionary society, we need not linger to explain. The result was on the one hand to assist in propping up the tottering fabric of society and on the other to rehabilitate mediaeval ideas on social relationships. To this influence can be attributed the combination, most marked in Southey, but noticeable

263

in many others, of pronounced Toryism with an outlook on social problems which put them far in advance of their more enlightened contemporaries. They did not become any the less Tories. The initial affiliations of the mediaeval revival may have been Whig, since the Parliamentarians of the seventeenth century had looked back beyond Tudor despotism to Lancastrian constitutionalism, but with Burke its true tendency becomes apparent. Conservatives, it has been said, put their golden age in the past; while those of progressive views look to a Utópia of the future. If we agree with this we shall understand why the influence of Rousseau with his state of nature proved in the long run conservative, and why the cult of mediaevalism also, in spite of its reforming aspect, is rightly classed among the forces of reaction.

Reaction, that is, more particularly against the eighteenth century. We have remarked above how, wearied by the intellectualism of the *philosophes*, men had thrown themselves back on authority, and how transcendentalism had offered them the categorical imperative, and Catholicism the Church. But the former had provided little satisfaction except to a few philosophers, and the latter was not a solution for Protestants with no infallible Church to fall back on. Their only resource was to take refuge from the demands of the future in the authority of the past. Now this could not be the immediate past, for historical development since the Renaissance and Reformation had led only too obviously up to the Enlightenment. Nor was classical antiquity much more acceptable. Not only was it non-Christian, it was also notoriously the idol of the eighteenth century, the pseudo-classical absurdities of which the Romantic movement did well not to attempt to emulate. On the other hand the Enlightenment had been supremely contemptuous of the Middle Ages. What appeal more suitable, then, than from an age of unbelief to the Ages of Faith, from an age of rebellion and self-assertion to the age of subordination and caste, from an age of the breaking of all bonds and loosening of all ties—social, moral and religious—to the age of fixed feudal hierarchy and unalterable law? Where else, too, should the reborn spirit of romance find inspiration and sympathy? These modern novelists, your Fielding and your Smollett, were all very well in their plain, prosaic way, but the new generation wanted heroic deeds, mystery, colour, and all the war-paint of romanticism. And the age found the first and greatest of Romantic novelists ready to supply its want.

Scott's novels no doubt intensified the mediaeval trend, but they did not call it into being in the first place. Thus it did not require the enchantments of the Wizard of the North to bring Southey under the spell of the Middle Ages. As early as 1803 he writes to Rickman, "Coleridge says there has never been a single line of common sense written about the dark ages. He was speaking of the knowledge and philosophy of that period; and I believe his assertion is true in a more extensive sense".(4) Southey, as soon as his conversion had been effected, took up feudalism with as much ardour as he had taken up Godwinism. He came to look on the disharmony in Europe as primarily a struggle "between the feudal system of society as variously modified throughout Europe, and the levelling principle of democracy"; in which struggle, he feared, the spirit of trade was gradually superseding the "rude but kindlier principle" of the feudal system. "Bad as the feudal times were, they were far less injurious than these commercial ones to the kindly and generous feelings of human nature, and far, far more favourable to the principles of honour and integrity." "While gain is the great object of pursuit, selfishness must ever be the uppermost feeling. I cannot dissemble from myself that it is the principle of our social system, and that it is awfully opposed to the spirit of Christianity."(5) The connection in Southey's mind between the revived cult of feudalism and a religious conception of society is obvious. Similarly, Wordsworth asks, "Why should not great landowners look for a substitute for what is lost of feudal paternity in the higher principles of christianized humanity and humble-minded brotherhood?"(6) Feudalism was not necessarily religious, nor Christianity feudal, but they both implied the same thing —that spirit of community life which Wordsworth and Southey assumed to have been lost in the anarchy of eighteenth-century individualism and the economic revolution and which it was their desire to see restored.

To what extent the Romantic writers were ignorant of the darker side of mediaeval life is difficult to say. Scott, at any rate, does not hesitate on occasion to deck his characters in sombre panoply and to hang his scenes with the trappings of sorrow and guilt. We need to be careful of exaggerating the prevalence of mediaeval barbarism: but though some very fine things can exist alongside the grossest brutality and superstition there can be no doubt that the Romantic school on the whole painted the Middle Ages in unjustifiably roseate hues.

However this may be, one of the best clues to the ideals of an age is the fiction it reads, because people do on the whole prefer to read not of what they are but of what they would like to be, not of their environment as it is, but of the environment in which they would like to be placed. Scott was the first to discover, or at least the first to exploit on a large scale, the mediaeval sentiment. It is consequently all the more significant that we can see in Scott, the high priest of mediaevalism himself, that the taste for the Middle Ages was more than a taste merely for a picturesque period of history. It was for certain things which could be found more particularly in the Middle Ages, it is true, but which could be found also in other fields. Was not feudal society supremely distinguished from modern by its recognition both in theory and practice of the value and significance of communal life, of the natural interdependence of individuals and of classes, and of the beauty of self-devotion to a corporate ideal? Not only in mediaeval Europe, but wherever he finds qualities such as these Sir Walter is at home. Does not his voice take on a new ring of spiritual exaltation when he comes to his Highland clans? The love of comradeship which had to be satisfied with drilling in the Volunteers, and the loyalty which could be bestowed on no worthier object than the Prince Regent, found in the devotion of clansmen to their clan and its chief a more stirring social relationship, even as he had found the same in mediaeval ties of allegiance and the code of chivalry.

Thus, to sum up, we see that the historic revival at this time amounted very largely to a revival of interest in the Middle Ages, and from Scott as well as from Coleridge and Southey we can see what it was that the Middle Ages gave them. We can see that they pass from the historic process of development to the implied subject of that process, to something in which are reconciled the principles of permanence and development, to something that is—over centuries and generations—

what the individual man is for some threescore years and ten—a body in which the elements are always changing without the body losing its identity, and which is the family, the clan, the city, the community, the nation. Behind religion, behind the historic idea itself, behind nationalism and the cry for social reform, the rediscovery of this is the root of all that is really new in the development of political theory at the end of the eighteenth and in the first decades of the nineteenth century, and *that* is the significance of the political thinking of Burke and Coleridge, Wordsworth, Southey, with Scott, Cobbett and a few lesser writers of their time.

III

CONCLUSION

We have arrived at what—it seems to us—is the ultimate significance in political thinking of the revolt against the eighteenth century, for we have discovered its definition of the State, in which, in a sense, all the rest is implied. It is one of the real definitions in which a science culminates, not one of the formal definitions in which it begins, and for Burke and the Lake Poets it is to be found in their idea of the national community. To attempt further to build up into a complete system the ideas we have analysed in this book would be to pass from the field of history to that of theory. In this matter the ideas of Burke and his followers must be left to speak for themselves without being artificially arranged into some system which their authors never had in mind when they evolved them. At the same time it will be worth our while in conclusion to emphasize what is the peculiar feature which distinguishes their political theory from other theories.

There have been, roughly speaking, two leading tendencies in political thinking—towards individualism and towards absolutism. Let us pass these rapidly under review. In the Middle Ages political theory proper did not exist. It came to birth in the form of absolutism with the development of the sovereign prince of the Renaissance and Reformation. The divine right of the mediaeval ruler persisted for a while in its new form, but the process which began with the attack on the authority of the Catholic Church of necessity could not end there. Divine right monarchs exhibited too few of the characteristics of divinity for their power to last once it had occurred to men to challenge it. As a final political result of the Protestant Reformation the sovereign prince was replaced by the sovereign individual, on whose behalf a theory of natural rights was elaborated by Locke. This culminated in the French Revolution and in economic individualism, and showed no further capacity for development, utilitarianism as a political doctrine being simply Lockian individualism with the assumptions of the pleasure-pain calculus put in place of the assumptions of natural law.

Before the Revolution, however, the absolutist theory had revived, although now with the sovereign State in place of the sovereign prince. The transition is to be observed in the political writings of Rousseau, who, beginning always with the abstract individual of the state of nature, ends with the General Will. Idealist philosophy took up the heritage of Rousseau, but whereas Rousseau certainly tried, if with doubtful success, to distinguish between the rules of political technology, the historical evolution, and the philosophical theory of the State, Idealism was too often content merely to identify them. With even more disastrous results, the philosophical desire for a closed system was allowed to result in an air of finality being given to the dialectical evolution traced out by Hegel, and so to the actual State as it was in his day. Unfortunately this meant the Kingdom of Prussia. Thus, under cover of the philosophical Absolute, all the evils of State absolutism—a very different matter—were sanctioned in an accentuated form.

These theories of the absolute State and of the absolute individual provided the twin bases of nineteenth-century politics, which are to a large extent vitiated by the fact that they spring in the ultimate resort from two extreme, untenable, and mutually incompatible principles. The attempt to work these theories out in practice has proved calamitous. The assertion of individual rights as such leads to anarchy, the attribution of all rights to the political State to tyranny, a practical inconvenience which is, of course, but a reflection of the theoretical weakness. The trouble with political theories based on the natural rights of the individual or on the absolute State, or on any combination of these two extremes, was that they were basing themselves on abstractions. The eighteenth-century "individual" was an invention of Locke. No one has ever isolated a natural man, and it would be of little use if anyone ever did: what the political theorist has to deal with is the individual in society. No government has, in fact, worked on the assumptions of natural man, and none ever could. More apparent practical success has been attained by the idea of the absolute State, but the results wherever men have attempted to put it into effect have been equally calamitous. No State has ever been able in fact to depend for its strength and cohesion merely on the exercise of sovereignty. Natural man and the sovereign State —the two conceptions from which most modern political thinking has sprung—are equally unreal and mischievous, because they arise not from observation and meditation on the facts of political society, but from the need to find theories which would justify claims to power.

It may be asked whether a less partial view of politics can be expected from Burke, who "to party gave up what was meant for mankind". The great advantage of Burke, however, was that he was not a professed political theorist; he was under no obligation to erect a theory at all, and he was therefore free from the artificial world of the system-makers. His position was more akin to that of the scientific observer, and as a practical politician he had unusual opportunities for studying the behaviour of man as a political animal. Similarly, the Lake Poets were merely students of the political life of their day, not professional dealers in theories. No previous political thinker, with the possible exception of Machiavelli, had been equally willing to start from the actual facts of human experience instead of from abstract ideas such as "sovereignty", "laws of nature", "natural man", "the felicific calculus", and the like.

Starting in this way from actual experience, they naturally found that the ultimate fact with which they had to deal, the basic material of politics, was neither the natural man nor the sovereign State, but simply individuals in society. The implication of this is that for political theory individuals must always be taken as they exist in society, on the one hand, and on the other, that political society is simply a feeling of relationship in the minds of individuals. This is the primary fact for the political theorist, who thus starts by assuming neither the rights of individuals nor the rights of the State. The recognition that neither of these are absolute rights lies at the base of all sound political thinking. So long as either the State or the individual was regarded as having absolute natural rights, no *modus vivendi* could be arranged between them, political speculation was doomed to oscillate vainly between anarchy and tyranny, and political practice could hope to see any abuse justified in the name of natural right. In declining to trace back all political right either to the State or to the individual, in acknowledging the priority of neither, Burke liberated political theory from the task of attempting to solve an insoluble problem.

How Burke's theory of the nature of the political relationship worked out in practice has been told at length in previous chapters. It was in essence a theory of nationality, because it founded itself on the historic unit called the nation, and neither on the State nor the individual, and it was destined to be followed by a widespread assertion of the claims of nationality in practice. The time has not yet come to pass judgment on a movement the possibilities of which for good and for evil have still to be exhausted. This we can say, that the theorists of the nation-state have been justified by the practical logic of events; for it has proved itself one of the strongest and most stable institutions in the world. Nations have been partitioned, suppressed for centuries, and out of the long historical memories of middle Europe have been born again. The whole fabric of society has been subverted and the nation has remained. Only, in speaking of Burke and his followers as theorists of the nation-state, we must be careful to point out that it is of the nation-state *minus*
272

the idea of sovereignty. To pass on to those who first recognized the fact of nationality any of the blame for the numerous excesses committed in its name would be patently unfair. The aggressive nationalism of a later day has taken over unchanged the heritage of the eighteenth-century despotisms—*corruptio optimi pessima*—but the aberrations of modern politics must not cause us to ignore the true fact of nationality.

The nature of the nation as a political body was first taught by Burke. Wordsworth re-echoes and deepens the call to the national spirit. Southey applies what is fundamentally the same idea to social problems. In Coleridge the attack on the eighteenth-century State finds its most unequivocal and philosophic exponent. He goes a long way towards building up a complete alternative system—and is perpetually frustrated by his own weakness and the spirit of the age. There was no doubt on which side this was. Burke's political theory has not even been given a distinguishing name. He founded no school, except in so far as the Lake Poets can be said to form one. Among Continental thinkers, despite occasional borrowings, the influence of his thought as a whole was negligible. And so the leaders of the first generation of romanticism died one by one, beaten and broken men, perishing among the spears of triumphant Victorianism, in which the individualist and utilitarian eighteenth century came finally into its own.

NOTES

I 1. Hume: Treatise on Human Nature, I. iii. 6.
   2. Id. I. iv. 1.
   3. Id. II. iii. 3.

4. Hume: Treatise on Human Nature, III. i. 1.
5. Id. III. i. 2.
6. Prelude, I. 340–4.

II 1. Vico: Scienza Nuova, II. i. 3.
2. C. Wordsworth: Memoirs of Wordsworth, II. 445
3. Essays, Moral and Political, I. 14.
4. Sel. Lett., I. 228, 1803.
5. Colloquies, I. 79; II. 414, 246–7, 250.
6. C. Wordsworth: Memoirs, II. 409.

BIBLIOGRAPHICAL NOTE

E. BURKE:

Works (8 vols.), Bohn's edition, 1873.
Speeches (4 vols.), 1816.
An account of the European Settlements in America, 1757.
History of the Present War, from the Annual Registers for 1758–61.
Annual Register, Historical Section, Vols. 1–30, 1758–88 (?).
Correspondence (4 vols.), 1844.
Selected Letters (ed. H. J. Laski), 1922.
Epistolary Correspondence of . . . Burke and Dr. French Laurence, 1822.
Correspondence of Burke and Windham, ed. J. P. Gilson, 1910.
Mr. Burke's Table Talk, Mrs. Crewe: Misc. Philobiblion Soc. Vol. VII.
T. Pownall: Administration of the Colonies, 1768, MS. notes by Burke (Br. Mus.).
Report of Committee of Secrecy, 1781, MS. notes by Burke (Br. Mus.).
A. P. I. Samuels: Early Life, Writings and Correspondence of Burke, 1923.

S. T. COLERIDGE:

Aids to Reflection (Bohn's ed.).
Anima Poetae, ed. E. H. Coleridge, 1895.
Biographia Epistolaris, ed. A. Turnbull, 1911.
Biographia Literaria (Bohn's ed.).
Constitution of Church and State, third ed., 1839.
Essays on Our Own Times, 1850.
The Friend, first edition, 1809–10.
The Friend, Second Version (third ed.), 1850
Lay Sermon (Bohn's ed.).
Literary Remains, 1836–9.
Notes, theological, political, and miscellaneous, 1853.
Poetical Works (Oxford ed.), 1912.
Statesman's Manual (Bohn's ed.)

S. T. COLERIDGE (*continued*):

Table Talk (Bohn's ed.).

Two Addresses on Sir Robert Peel's Bill, ed. Gosse, 1913.

Letters, ed. E. H. Coleridge, 1895.

Letters, Conversations and Recollections of Coleridge: Alsopp, 1864.

Unpublished Letters: J. P. Estlin (Philobiblion Soc., Vol. 15).

Letters, hitherto uncollected, ed. W. F. Prideaux, 1913.

MS. notes by Coleridge in books at the British Museum.

J. T. Haney: A bibliography of Coleridge, 1903.

T. J. Wise: A bibliography of Coleridge, and Supplement, 1913.

R. SOUTHEY:

Colloquies on Society, 1829.

Essays, Moral and Political, 1832.

Journal of a Tour to the Netherlands, 1902.

Letters from England, Espriella, 1807.

Life and Correspondence, ed. C. C. Southey (6 vols.), 1849–50.

Selected Letters, ed. J. W. Warter (4 vols.), 1856.

W. WORDSWORTH:

Poetical Works, ed. Hutchinson, 1916.

Prose Works, ed. W. Knight, 1896.

Grosart: Prose Works of Wordsworth, Vol. III. Sec. III. Reminiscences, 1876.

Letters of the Wordsworth Family (3 vols.), ed. W. Knight, 1907.

INDEX